Engineering
the City

How Infrastructure Works

Projects and Principles for Beginners

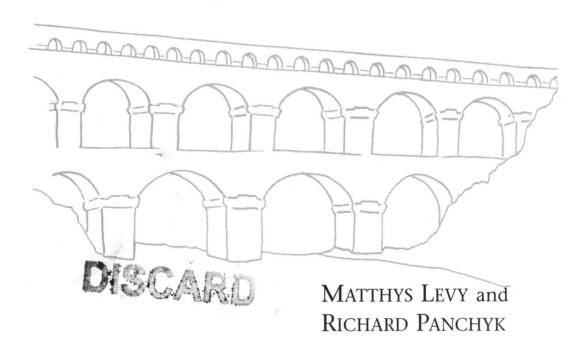

MATTHYS LEVY and
RICHARD PANCHYK

CHICAGO
REVIEW
PRESS

Library of Congress Cataloging-in-Publication Data

Levy, Matthys.
    Engineering the city : how infrastructure works : projects and principles for beginners / Matthys Levy and Richard Panchyk.
        p. cm.
    Includes bibliographical references and index.
    ISBN 1-55652-419-6
    1. Civil engineering—Juvenile literature. 2. Municipal engineering—Juvenile literature. [1. Civil engineering. 2. Municipal engineering.] I. Panchyk, Richard. II. Title.
    TA 149.L49 2000
    624-dc21

                                                        00-031774

This book is dedicated to Nicola Freeman, Matthew William Panchyk, and to all children who ask "why?"

Table of Contents

Acknowledgments

We would first like to thank Lorraine Whitman, the executive director of the Salvadori Center, for organizing a focus group of teachers to read, comment on, and make suggestions for improving the book. Many of their suggestions were extremely valuable and helped us raise the quality and usefulness of the book. We also want to thank teachers Jamil Azim, Manette Gampel, Ken Harris, Francis Osei, and Bernard Winter for their efforts and constructive criticism and thank Julia Goldschmidt for compiling notes of the focus group sessions. We also appreciated the support provided for the focus groups by the Institute for Civil Infrastructure Systems (ICIS) at New York University's Robert F. Wagner Graduate School of Public Service (funded by NSF). Finally, we would like to thank our editor, Cynthia Sherry, for having faith!

Engineering
the City

Introduction

Imagine that you lived in a place where there were no pipes to carry water to your faucet and your toilet, no pipes to carry away your waste, no wires to power your appliances and computers and to light your home, no wires to carry your telephone conversations and your Internet messages, no roads on which to drive, no railroad tracks to guide trains, and no bridges to cross rivers. Would that be a place where you would want to live? We are certain you answered "no" and rejected the idea of living without *infrastructure*. You certainly see roads every day, and you have seen railroad tracks and perhaps telephone and power wires suspended from wooden poles. But much of the infrastructure of the city or town or village in which you live is invisible; the pipes and wires are usually buried underground or hidden behind walls. The power plant that supplies electricity through your wires is often so far away that it might as well be on another world. The reservoirs that collect the water you need are usually hidden in the hills far from where you live.

The story of infrastructure teaches us about the history of human development from the time we lived in caves and first set out to establish villages. It also shows us the contribution of science, mathematics, and industry to our built environment. As you read this book, we hope you begin to appreciate the contribution of the invisible infrastructure to the quality of your life. We learned a lot and had fun writing it and hope you enjoy reading it.

1

Water, Water Everywhere

There would be no life without water. As we look up to the heavens and particularly toward our nearest neighbors, the planets, one of our first questions is usually: Is there any water there? For centuries, the lines crisscrossing the surface of Mars that can be seen through a telescope were thought to be canals, perhaps constructed by intelligent beings. Sadly, this turns out not to be true. When a spacecraft landed on Mars recently and sent back signals that water may exist under the surface of the red planet, astrophysicists, scientists who study the composition of the universe, were wildly excited. It was the first evidence that life may exist outside of Earth. The first clue that other forms of life exist somewhere in the universe will most likely be the existence of water—the building block of life.

What Is Water?

Although water is a liquid, it is a compound of two gases: one part oxygen mixed with two parts hydrogen. If you look at a globe of Earth, you will notice that the color blue predominates. Blue is typically used to designate water, which covers 71 percent of the globe. This ocean water tastes salty and contains as many as 32 different salts and minerals. If you were to drink it, you would get sick. Actually, too much saltwater could easily kill you. On the other hand, if you were to put a fish from the ocean into fresh water, it would swell up (by a process called endosmosis) and die. Fortunately for us, seawater is heated by the sun and evaporates, leaving all the salts and minerals behind. It then condenses into clouds that float around the sky and, through precipitation, release their water as rain or snow (Figure 1.1). When rain or snow falls on the land, it seeps into the ground and forms springs, rivers, and lakes that all, eventually, flow back into the ocean. The water that we use comes from these springs, rivers, or lakes and is relatively pure. This cycle of evaporation, condensation, precipitation, seepage, and flow is the *natural water cycle* without which life on Earth would not be possible.

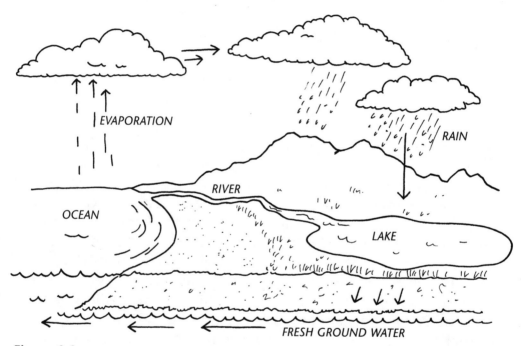

Figure 1.1

The First People

Even the earliest humanlike creatures, called Australopithecines, who lived 4,000,000 years ago, knew how and where to find water. When our human ancestors first left their cave dwellings more than 10,000 years ago (at the end of the Ice Age or Paleolithic period), they gathered in villages located near streams, rivers, or lakes. They recognized that water was their most important commodity. After all, about 70 percent (actually somewhere between 67 and 78 percent) of the human body consists of water that must constantly be replaced.

Water in the body is used to help drive the digestive system, to lubricate the body's joints, to cushion the internal organs, to cleanse the body both inside and out, and to control the skin's temperature through evaporation as we perspire.

Our ancestors usually sited their dwellings close to water. From their round huts of woven vines or reeds covered with thatch, these early people looked out onto a river or lake and drank its water, washed in it, and pulled out buckets of it to irrigate their gardens.

Three thousand years ago, on the banks of the Danube River and the lakes of Switzerland, Stone Age civilizations of hunters and agriculturists built platforms on poles set into the river or lake bottom. On these platforms, they built clay floors with raised hearths. They framed their houses with steep thatch roofs and triangular gables and walls of mud plaster or logs sharpened to fit into vertical grooved posts (Figure 1.2). From these houses, the people would lift buckets of water from the river or lake for their drinking and cooking needs. They would also dump their waste down to the lake or river.

Figure 1.2

At that time, no one thought of separating the drinking water from that used for cleaning. After all, the lake was so large or the river so swift that one person or even a family couldn't possibly become ill

WATER POLLUTION

When water is polluted or contaminated it contains things besides oxygen and hydrogen. Pour some water into a glass and look at its color. Is it clear, with no particles floating about? Does it have an odor? Polluted water often has the acrid smell of ammonia, the same liquid that is used for cleaning. Sometimes, however, polluted water looks perfectly clear because the offending bacteria are too small to be visible. To be perfectly safe, always have water from a new source tested in a laboratory before drinking it.

from drinking the same water in which one washed.

However, the first families multiplied over time. The village became a town and, much later, a city. After a while, the crystal-clear lake or river gradually turned cloudy and people became ill from drinking its smelly water.

People noticed that water that flowed from a spring in the ground was usually clear. So they began to dig *wells* in the ground as deep as necessary to find this clear water (Figure 1.3). Water that flows into wells originates as rain or snow that seeps underground through the earth, which acts as a filter to remove danger-ous organisms.

Since older wells were dug by hand, they were made about 3 feet (1 m) in diameter, just big enough for a man to stand in the hole while digging it. These early wells were lined with stone to keep earth from falling into the hole. The Indus Valley in present-day Pakistan had this type of well

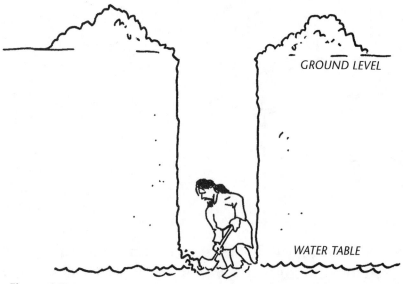

GROUND LEVEL

WATER TABLE

Figure 1.3

5,000 years ago. Later civilizations used clay bricks to line their wells (Figure 1.4). Today wells are dug by machine and are no bigger than the 2- to 4-inch (50- to 100-mm) diameter steel pipe that is drilled into the ground. Since modern drills can go through rock as well as soil, wells can recover water that flows through cracks in the rock hundreds of feet below the surface.

WHAT IS HARD WATER?

Sometimes, as water passes through the earth, it picks up salts of calcium and magnesium. You can identify hard water by boiling it in a pot and noticing that a white, crusty residue forms on the inside of the pot.

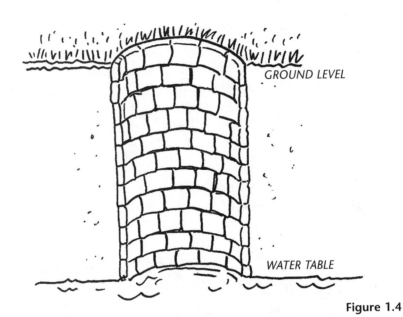

GROUND LEVEL

WATER TABLE

Figure 1.4

The type of earth or rock through which underground water flows limits the amount of water that flows into a well. To supply water to larger families and villages, larger and deeper wells were needed. Such town wells can still be seen in the central squares of many old villages in Europe and Asia.

Many towns today rely on wells for their water supply. But these wells reach down past several layers of soil, sand, and gravel into what is called an *aquifer*, or layer of porous, water-holding rock. These aquifers were originally pure, but as people used fertilizers and chemicals on their land, the chemicals began to seep down into the

THE FIRST AQUEDUCT

Fourteen hundred years ago the Greek engineer Eupalinus of Megara was given the task of supplying water to the city of Samos. To accomplish this, he built one of the first aqueducts dug through a mountain. The tunnel was almost 3,300 feet (1,000 m) long and was dug simultaneously from both sides of the mountain. When the two crews digging the tunnel met in the middle, the centerline of each side was only 16 feet (5 m) off, a miracle since they had no instruments capable of accurately measuring angles.

aquifers. Thousands of wells all over the world are now too polluted to drink from. Only the deepest aquifers remain unpolluted today.

Eventually, even in ancient times, villages grew to the size of towns whose increasing population needed more water than wells could supply. "Why not bring the water down from mountain springs?" thought the people of these ancient civilizations. But first a problem had to be solved: because water only flows downhill, how do you create a channel that slopes from the mountain spring down to the city, crossing hills and valleys? An *aqueduct*, a conduit, originally lined in stone, provided the answer. To cross valleys, arched bridges were built (Figure 1.5); and to penetrate hills, tunnels were bored. The first aqueducts were built almost 3,000 years ago in the countries around the Mediterranean Sea. Although they were not the first aqueduct

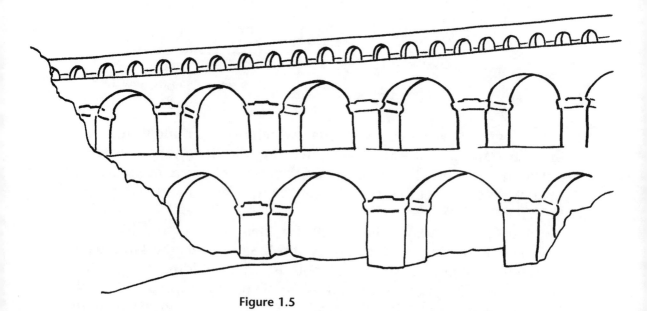

Figure 1.5

builders, the clever Romans developed the idea masterfully, building many stone aqueducts to supply the cities of their growing empire. For instance, there were 11 aqueducts leading into ancient Rome with a total length of 310 miles (500 km) of which 260 miles (420 km) were in tunnels and the rest in arched structures. These satisfied the needs of the city's occupants for domestic use, public baths, and almost 200 public fountains. They were so well built that many of Rome's aqueducts survive today, although underground pipes have replaced their function.

Find the Centerline

Discover what it was like for early engineers to build straight tunnels. Try this experiment with four friends!

MATERIALS
- **2 empty cans**
- **2 short sticks**
- **Blindfold**
- **Lots of pebbles, pennies, paper clips, or other objects to use for markers**

Give two of your friends each an empty can and a short stick. Have them stand in opposite corners of a room or outside on a lawn. Next, blindfold them and make certain they don't peek. Be sure to tell them to be silent. Turn them around a few times so they don't know which way they are facing. Ask each of them to start walking slowly and at the same time hit their tin cans every 10 seconds. Explain to them that they should walk toward the sound of the other can. Have two other friends walk behind each of the first two, marking with pebbles (or any other small objects) the paths being followed. The game ends when the first two friends reach each other.

Notice the path followed by each of the two as they walked toward each other using only sound as their cue. See how difficult it is to follow a straight line.

Aqueducts are still built today to feed cities' need for water. Instead of stone, modern aqueducts are built of sealed pipes of steel or concrete reinforced with steel bars. These pipes are strong enough to withstand the pressure of the water pushing against their sides, and are usually circular except when they sit on the ground.

How the Pressure Exerted by Water Shapes Conduits

MATERIALS
- **Flexible plastic tube with soft sides and a sealed end, or a long, thin balloon**
- **Water**
- **Duct tape or electrical tape**

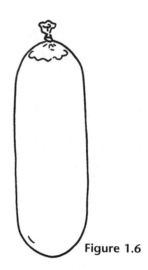

Figure 1.6

🏛 Fill the tube or balloon with water and hold vertically. If you use a balloon, don't fill it to bursting. Close the open end by tying or taping it. Notice that the shape of the tube is circular (Figure 1.6). Now lay the tube on a table and notice what shape it takes. Compare it to the drawing of the Croton Aqueduct, built in 1842 to provide water to New York City (Figure 1.7).

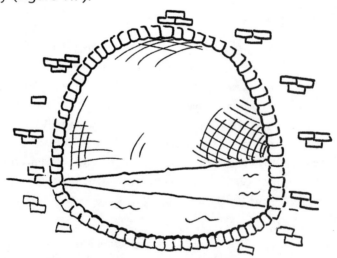

Figure 1.7

Instead of sloping continually from the water source to the city, modern steel or concrete aqueducts can follow the terrain of the land. They are able to do this because they are sealed and because they take advantage of the *siphon* principle, discovered by Hero, a Greek who lived around 150 B.C. Hero found that he could make water flow uphill in a sealed tube. Of course, there was a trick involved in his method.

How Does a Siphon Work?

MATERIALS

- **2 cooking pots or large containers to hold water**
- **Water**
- **Chair**
- **Rubber or plastic tube, or piece of clean, small-diameter garden hose about 3 feet (1 m) long**

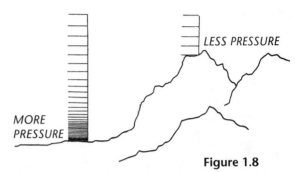

Figure 1.8

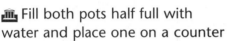 Fill both pots half full with water and place one on a counter and the other on a chair below the counter. Take the tube (make sure it is long enough to reach from the counter to the chair) and place one end in the upper pot. Take the other end in your mouth and suck until water rises up in the tube. Now pinch the tube to keep the water from sliding back into the upper pot and place the open end of the tube into the lower pot. Release the tube and notice that water flows from the upper to the lower pot. In doing so, water first has to flow up the tube (to get over the edge of the pot) before it flows down the other end. This only works if the second pot is below the first one (this is the trick). What do you think causes water to flow uphill? Is it any different than sucking liquid through a straw?

The scientific explanation is that the air all around us exerts *pressure*, a force acting on every square inch (mm) of surface it touches. This air pressure represents the weight of the column of air above the earth's surface all the way up to the stratosphere. Since the air becomes thinner—and therefore lighter—the higher we go, the air pressure is less on the top of a mountain than it is in the valley (Figure 1.8).

As we suck on a straw, we are removing the air in the straw (creating a vacuum) and allowing the outside air pressure to push the liquid up the straw. This is the same action that takes place in the siphon. It is also the same action that takes place as a pump pulls water up from a well. Unfortunately, there is a limit to how high the water can be lifted in a siphon. When the outside air pressure equals the weight of the column of water in the tube, the water can go no higher. This happens when the tube of water is about 33 feet (10 m) above the surface of the upper water reservoir at sea level (and less if it is on the top of a mountain where air pressure is lower).

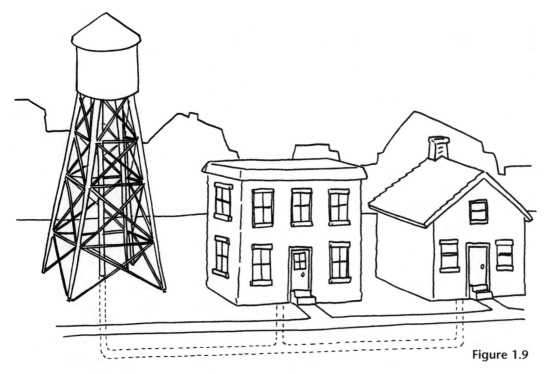

Figure 1.9

In places where water is obtained from underground aquifers more than 30 feet (10 m) below the ground, pumps must be placed at the bottom of the wells. Instead of sucking up the water, the pumps push the water up the pipe. Such pumps can operate hundreds of feet below the ground.

Many towns have storage tanks on top of towers that are higher than the highest building (Figure 1.9). Water can flow from the storage tank down a pipe, through an underground pipe, and then back

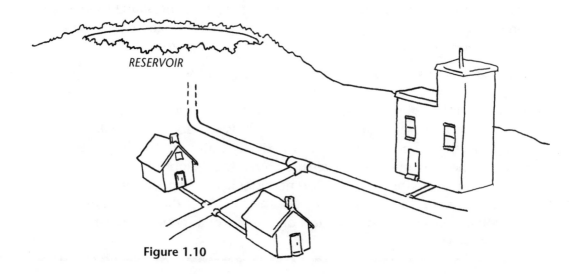

RESERVOIR

Figure 1.10

up to the top floor of any building in town. Under a modern city a maze of pipes distributes water from the reservoir, or storage tank, through large pipes and then smaller pipes to the thousands of buildings in which we work and live (Figure 1.10).

Next time you turn on a faucet, imagine how far the water has traveled and through what aqueducts or pipes and from what reservoirs or storage tanks.

We have come a long way from being able to sip clear water from streams and rivers. In most places, water is treated with the chemical chlorine to purify it before it enters our homes. Where the untreated water is not very safe, the chlorine taste can be pretty strong, but it won't do you any harm. In some towns, fluoride is also added to the water. Fluoride is a chemical that is good for our teeth and helps prevent cavities.

Although the water we use may come from far away, thanks to our high-technology testing and treatment systems, most of the water that comes into our homes is safe to drink.

Infrastructure Activities

🏛 Draw a time line showing the dates when events identified in this chapter took place. A time line is a linear graph that you divide into parts (years, in this case) on which you identify significant events.

🏛 Think about how the ideas in this chapter apply to the workings of your body. What organs or organ systems most closely relate to the story of water? Write your ideas down in a journal or notebook.

🏛 Find out where the water you use in your house comes from. Does it come from a reservoir, well, or river? How far away is the source? In some places water may come from a lake or the ocean. In Chicago, for instance, water is pumped from Lake Michigan through a filtration plant where chemicals are added to purify the water. In Kuwait, on the Arabian Gulf, water is pumped from the ocean through a desalinization plant that removes the salts and purifies the water.

2 Water Transportation

The story of cities starts with water. As you have seen in the previous chapter, early people settled along bodies of water such as streams, rivers, or lakes. These early settlements grew, and many became cities. If you were asked to name the great cities in your country and the world, you would certainly mention a city along a river or lake. For example, Rome is on the Tiber, Paris is on the Seine, London is on the Thames, New York City is on the Hudson, and Cairo is on the Nile.

Cities and Water

MATERIALS
- **World map**
- **Highlighter**
- **Pencil**
- **Paper**

On your map, use your highlighter to draw lines along the rivers and around lakes. Now identify cities that lie along the waterways and write a list of the largest ones and their respective countries. You will notice that it is almost impossible to find a major city that is not next to or near a body of water. A city such as Las Vegas that is far from any body of water is totally dependent on water being piped down from faraway mountain reservoirs.

The earliest people probably didn't know much about what existed beyond the immediate area in which they lived and hunted. For them, leaving the immediate neighborhood was probably almost as frightening as being visited by strangers. But as cities developed almost 7,000 years ago, their occupants began to travel outside their immediate environs. There were many reasons for them to look beyond their city's borders. They had to find agricultural land to feed a growing population; they needed natural resources such as iron and copper to make tools and containers; and they wanted to expand their influence to other cities or peoples. When people built up their courage and decided to explore the world beyond their territory, it was natural for them to think of using rivers as roads. But to travel on the river they first needed boats.

Papyrus reeds grew along the banks of the Nile River in ancient Egypt. These plants, which are now extinct in lower Egypt, grew to heights of up to 13 feet (4 m) and were truly miraculous in their usefulness. The root was used as fuel and in the manufacture of utensils. Its pith, the soft core of the stem, was used as food. The whole stem was used to make boats, sails, mats, cloth, and cords or ropes. But the name of the plant suggests its most important use, making paper.

To make paper, the Egyptians first peeled the papyrus reed to remove the outer rind. The inner part was then cut into strips, soaked in water, and placed in two layers, one perpendicular to the other. This sheet was then covered with a linen cloth and pressed with stones or hammered with a mallet. After drying, the sheet was smoothed out and rolled up into a scroll. Today, paper is made from tree pulp, cotton, or other fibrous materials and is prepared in a manner similar to that used by the Egyptians.

The Egyptians used their papyrus boats (Figure 2.1) to trade, travel, fish, and carry armies to war. Since these papyrus boats were rather flimsy, they were used primarily to travel up and down the Nile. The Egyptians did not at first venture into the more dangerous waters of the Mediterranean Sea. These papyrus boats are so ancient that the Bible refers to them. Isaiah called them "vessels of bulrushes."

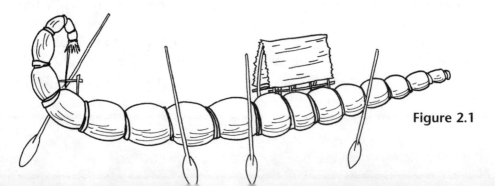

Figure 2.1

Why Do Boats Float?

MATERIALS
- Assorted small blocks of wood, pieces of Styrofoam, stones, metal (a paper clip or coin), and pieces of plastic
- Medium-sized bowl filled with water
- Kitchen scale

Drop your various items into the bowl of water and see which ones float and which ones sink.

Now, take out a stone and a block of wood. Place each on a scale and record their weights. You will now determine the volume of both the stone and the wood block. In the case of a wood block with square corners, measure its width, w, its height, h, and its depth, d. The volume is w x h x d. Since the stone does not have regular dimensions, you will need to use a clever idea conceived by a Greek scientist who lived 2,300 years ago.

Archimedes was asked by King Hieron to find out if a crown was made of pure gold or of silver with a thin gold veneer. One day he noticed that when he stepped into a bath, the volume of water that overflowed equaled the volume of his body. He was so excited that he ran naked through the streets of Syracuse, where he lived, yelling, "Eureka!" which means "I have found it." Archimedes had realized this meant that if he weighed the displaced volume of water he would know the density of a body. Applying this principle to the question of the crown—since gold is denser than silver- he could determine if the crown was pure gold. He submerged the crown in a pail of water that was full to the top. He collected all the water that spilled out and poured it into a cup. He then weighed the crown on a balance scale, placing pure gold coins on the other side of the balance. Finally, he tossed the gold coins in a topped-off water pail and poured the water that spilled out into another cup. He then compared the amount of water in the two cups. Do you think that when Archimedes put the gold-plated silver crown into a pail of water it displaced more or less water than the equally heavy pure gold coins?

The answer is more, because a pure gold crown will displace less water than a silver crown of equal weight.

You can now use Archimedes' idea to determine the volume of the stone by pouring the displaced water into a measuring cup. To convert the amount of displaced water, which is measured in ounces, into cubic inches, divide the number of fluid ounces by .554. One cubic inch equals .554 fluid ounces. The volume of the stone can now be expressed in cubic inches.

The reason a particular material floats is that its density (weight of a unit volume of the material) is less than the weight of an equal volume of water. This is the principle of buoyancy. So a heavier piece of wood (low density) will float, while a lighter metal coin (high density) would not float. To obtain the density of the wood or stone, divide its weight by its volume. The result can be compared to the density of water, 0.554 ounces per cubic inch (1 g/cc), to determine which will float and which will sink.

Even a heavy material can float if it is shaped to displace water; canoes and boats have been made with shells of concrete or steel. The Native Americans built many different kinds of canoes. Some were made of a light wooden frame with pieces of tree bark sewn onto it. In northern climates canoes were built with driftwood frames held together with sinew, which are strips of animal tendon, and were covered with animal skins. Driftwood was used because in the far north there were no trees, so the natives used the wood that floated ashore. These boats were made waterproof by rubbing animal fat into the skins. They weighed as little as 33 pounds (15 kg), making them easily transportable across stretches of ice or land.

Boat building developed in different ways in different parts of the world. The earliest boats were rafts, made of tree trunks tied together (Figure 2.2). They were the simplest boats, but certainly not the fastest. Hollowed-out tree trunks (dugouts) were the first real boats, followed by canoes and larger boats that had the same shape but were made of strips of wood attached to a frame (Figure 2.3). Often these

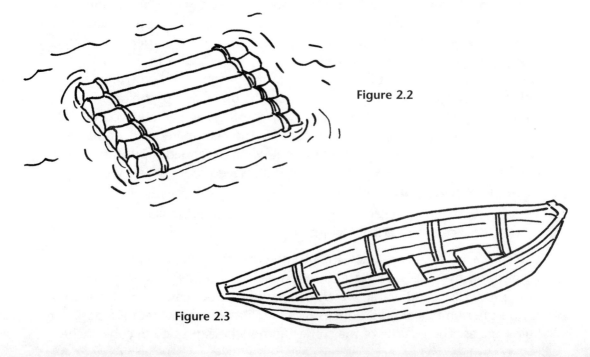

Figure 2.2

Figure 2.3

WHAT IS THE BEST SHAPE FOR A BOAT?

You can test this in a tub of water by first pushing the water with the flat of your hand. Then turn your hand so it slices through the water. Notice that you need more force to push the water than to slice it. This tells you two things. First, water has more compressive strength (when you pushed it) than shear strength (when you sliced through it). In fact, water has no shear strength. Second, a boat will move more easily if it is shaped to cut through the water. This is why boats usually have a tapered bow, the front part of the boat (Figure 2.4).

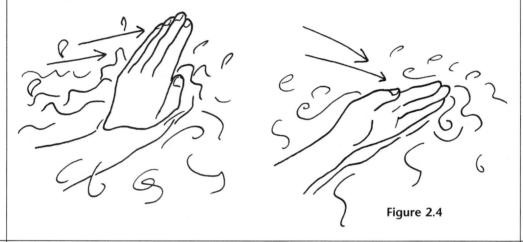

Figure 2.4

strips of wood were coated to make them waterproof. The ancient Egyptians used a paste made from the pith of the papyrus reed to waterproof their boats.

Today there are two basic boat shapes: flat-bottomed and tapered. Flat-bottomed boats are used for fishing or slow travel on smooth water. Their shape helps them float on the surface of the water, but it makes them less stable in stormy weather. Like a tree with no roots, a flat-bottomed boat has nothing anchoring it in the water for stability (Figure 2.5).

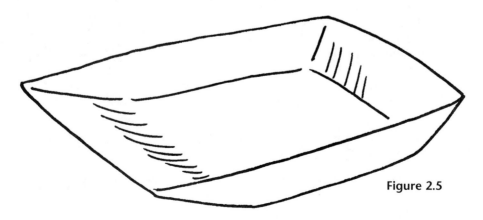

Figure 2.5

Tapered boat shapes are made to shear through the water for faster travel. Really fast boats have a tapered bow and a flattened stern, the back part of the boat (Figure 2.6). When these boats go very fast, their bows rise up above the surface of the water and they skim along on their flattened sterns, which is called planing.

Figure 2.6

Introducing iron or brass to join the wooden planks together enabled larger boats to be built—boats that could be taken out to the ocean. Nevertheless, the Egyptians still used papyrus to seal the joints between the planks so they would not leak. Now transportation could extend well beyond the city and even the country.

THE KON TIKI

In 1947, the anthropologist Thor Heyerdahl wanted to prove that the people of Polynesia, located in the South Pacific, arrived there by sailing from South America. He built a raft by tying together nine large bamboo logs and putting a small bamboo cabin on top of it. With five other adventurers and a supply of food, including 684 boxes of pineapple, he set sail from the coast of Peru on the raft he called the Kon Tiki (Figure 2.7). After crossing 4,300 miles (7,000 km) of ocean in 101 days, he arrived in Polynesia satisfied that the island's forebears could have completed the same voyage 1,500 years earlier.

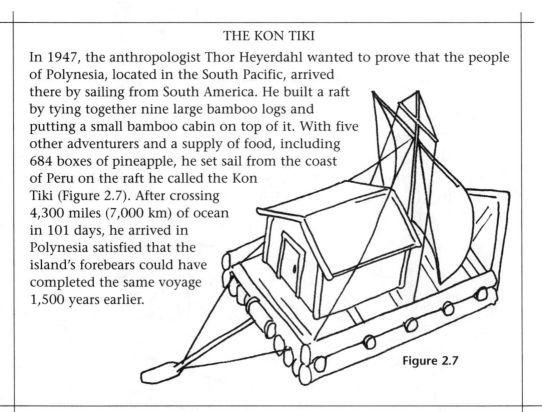

Figure 2.7

As more boats were used to move people and goods, it became necessary to develop harbors, docks, and piers where the boats could load and unload their cargo as well as their passengers. The water in the harbor had to be deep enough so that the boat coming alongside the dock would not touch the bottom and become stuck. The first harbors near the ocean were natural ones, with deep water and protection from waves. The ancient harbor of Ostia, the gateway to Rome, Italy, was adequate for a while but needed more protection from the waves. Consequently, a semicircular wall of stone was built out into the sea. It kept out the worst waves but proved inadequate since boats were still rocked about inside the wall. Fifty years after the first wall (called a breakwater) was completed, the Emperor Trajan improved it so that no waves could penetrate into the harbor by building a second wall in front of the opening in the first wall (Figure 2.8).

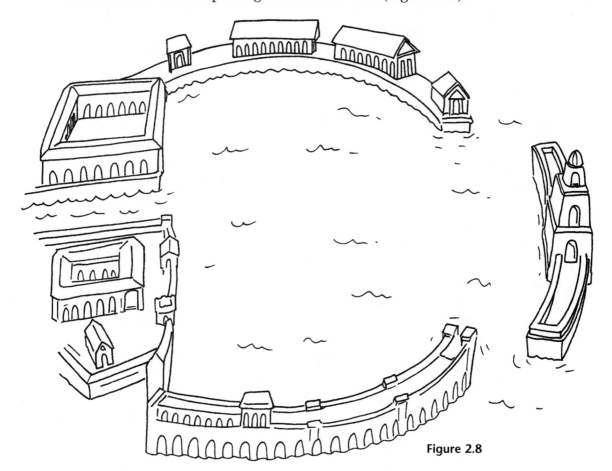

Figure 2.8

On the other hand, some older ports were abandoned and some have disappeared as the boundary between land and sea has changed over time. For instance, the ancient Greek port city of Ephesus (located on the coast of modern-day Turkey) is now some distance from the sea. The Belgian city of Brugge also used to connect to the sea. When its link to the sea filled with mud and silt, Brugge lost its power and wealth.

To travel across the oceans, boats, which were at first small, became ships, which are big—often bigger than some of the ancient cities. Larger harbors were developed for those cities located along the coast of the world's oceans: New York City, United States; Sydney, Australia; Hong Kong, China; Marseilles, France; Tokyo, Japan. How many cities can you identify on a map that have major harbors?

Barges, which are really large flat-bottomed boats, were the simplest vessels to carry great volumes of goods such as grains, coal, and ore. Until well into the late 19th century, roads were rough and vehicles that could travel on them were small. Barges could be built large and were able to travel on smooth water. Rivers soon became crowded with barges moving material all along their lengths. But if there was no river, it was not possible to cross the land except by unloading the barge, loading many smaller wagons, and traveling to the next river where another barge could be loaded with the goods. This was a very inefficient way to manage goods. Someone thought of a clever idea: Why not cut a *canal* between the two rivers? There were many problems with this idea. The land was rarely flat between the two rivers, and there were often hills to cross. When a proposal was put forward in the early 19th century to dig a canal 363 miles (581 kilometers) long between the city of Albany on the Hudson River and Buffalo on Lake Erie, even Thomas Jefferson, the former president and a great inventor, thought it impossible. For one thing, Albany, New York, is hundreds of feet (meters) lower than Buffalo, New York, and then there are hills between the two cities! To solve these two problems, the builders divided the length of the canal into sections, each at a different elevation. Between each section they used *locks*.

Locks were developed in China in the 10th century and in Holland in the 13th century. A lock is a section of a canal with gates at either end (Figure 2.9). When one gate at the lower level is opened, a boat can enter and the gate is then closed behind it. Water is then allowed to flow into the lock from the next, higher, section of the canal. When the water in the lock reaches the same level as that in

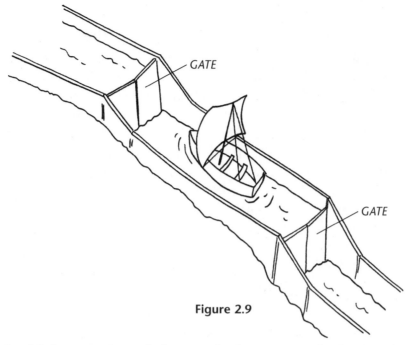

Figure 2.9

the higher section of the canal, the gate at the higher level is opened and the boat exits the lock. A reverse procedure is used when traveling in the other direction with the water from the lock flowing into the lower level.

A total of 83 locks were needed to connect the Hudson River and Lake Erie. When the canal was completed, boats could travel from New York City all the way to Chicago by crossing through the Great Lakes and, after another, smaller, canal was dug, to the Mississippi River. This meant that boats could travel on rivers and canals all the way from New York City to New Orleans and the Gulf of Mexico. This system was an important part of

THE GRAND CANAL
China's Grand Canal, built between 485 B.C. and A.D. 283, links the cities of Tianjin and Hangzhou and was used to help collect taxes in the form of rice grain. Today, along its 1,054-mile (1,700-km) length, you can see small barges as well as oceangoing ships.

the nation's transportation network. Look at a map of the United States and highlight all the rivers, inland waterways, and canals. You will discover that there are more than 25,000 miles (40,000 km) of navigable waterways with over 200 locks in various locations.

Over time, canals were built in every part of the world including Belgium, France, England, China, and Greece. The early canals connected waterways that were almost at the same elevation since locks had not yet been invented. However, even these canals sometimes had to cross a mountain. Instead of going around the mountain, some canals went into tunnels that were dug through the mountain. Where a canal had to cross a valley, it was raised up like an aqueduct—many still exist today. Both tunnels and aqueducts continue to be used even after the invention of locks since it is sometimes easier to travel at one level rather than having to go up and down (Figure 2.10).

The two most important canals in use today connect not rivers but oceans. The Panama Canal in Central America, completed in 1914, connects the Atlantic and Pacific Oceans, shortening by thousands of miles the route ships previously had to follow by going around the tip

Figure 2.10

of South America. The Suez Canal between the Mediterranean Sea and the Arabian Gulf, completed in 1869, avoided the long and dangerous voyage that ships traveling between Europe and Asia had taken around the southern tip of Africa. A smaller version of this canal was actually built 4,000 years ago by the ancient Egyptians but had long ago been abandoned.

Another development helped water become a major means of transportation—the invention of the steam engine, which would power boats of all kinds.

How Does Steam Power an Engine?

MATERIALS
- 1 piece of facial tissue
- 1 long dowel or stick, 18 inches (500 mm) long
- Water
- 2 small cooking pots, one with a lid

ADULT SUPERVISION RECOMMENDED.

Figure 2.11

Poke the tissue onto the end of the dowel or stick about $1/3$ of the way from any edge. Pour equal amounts of water to fill the pots $2/3$ full. Place a lid on one pot and leave the other uncovered. Place the two pots on the stove and heat the water to boiling. Turn off the stove and observe the steam rising from the uncovered pot. Dangle the tissue on the stick a few inches over the pot without the lid and observe how it moves (Figure 2.11). Now, have an adult carefully remove the lid of the other pot as you dangle the tissue over it (Figure 2.12). Observe the difference?

Figure 2.12

The scientific explanation is that there are two conditions that give steam its power—small, enclosed space and high heat. First, remember that the steam in the pot with the lid had no place to go and so, when the lid was removed, it seemed a lot more forceful. As molecules (tiny particles) in the water are heated, they move faster. Since heat rises, when the lid was lifted, the steam molecules rushed out and moved the tissue.

Steam pipes used to heat your house operate by the same principle—hot air and steam rise, so the boiler is usually in the basement, and the steam is carried through narrow pipes to radiators throughout the house.

Second, as boiling water gets hotter, it creates more and more steam. In a steam engine, the steam is superheated, which means that it gets so hot that the excited molecules have tremendous force. As the steam is released into an engine chamber, the force pushes pistons back and forth. This sideways motion is converted by means of an eccentric arm into a circular motion, which is then used to turn a paddle wheel or propeller on a steamboat.

Steamboats were especially popular during the 19th and early 20th centuries. No longer did people have to depend on human strength (rowing) or the wind (sailing) to get from one place to another. Only when other forms of transportation (especially the train) became popular did the steamship die out.

If you live along a river or in a port city, you can still see ships and barges of all kinds transporting goods but not nearly as many as in the past. Other forms of transportation, trains, trucks, and airplanes, have taken over to move goods faster and more economically. But bulky or heavy goods such as oil, cars, coal, and metals are still shipped by boat.

Infrastructure Activities

ADULT SUPERVISION RECOMMENDED.

Build a boat that will support your weight using only heavy packing tape and a sheet of corrugated cardboard 5 x 7 feet (1.5 m x 2.1 m). Try this experiment only in shallow water. To determine the best possible shape and configuration, first experiment with a light cardboard model in a bathtub. Experiment with boat shapes and note which are more stable when you put them in the tub. If you manage to build a boat that supports your weight you will realize that shape and rigidity are the two most important characteristics for boat construction.

Make a list of goods, such as clothes, appliances, and furniture, in your home or school and note where they were made (look at the label or tag). Which ones do you think were transported by ship?

3
Irrigation

To grow plants, which can be used for food, fuel, and building materials, you need water. Unfortunately, water may not be located everywhere it is needed. Northern California, for instance, has a lot of rain and many rivers and lakes with plentiful fresh water, but its weather is cool and often cloudy. On the other hand, southern California has abundant sunshine, is warm, and has many people living there who want to drink, bathe, wash their cars, and grow food, but it is dry and has little water. How can the people of southern California get the water they need? Also, how can they get the water they need when they need it? Here, then, are two problems: water is often in the wrong place, and water, falling as rain or snow, often appears at the wrong time.

The clever people of ancient Egypt faced this same problem and developed a solution that we still use today. They learned to *irrigate*, that is, to bring the water to the land where and when it is needed. Egypt is sliced in two by the great Nile valley, a region sandwiched between two deserts that are constantly trying to move in and overrun it. Yet the land of the valley is rich and fertile and bathed in sunlight that warms its many crops of fruit and grain. The fertility of this arid land is possible because of irrigation.

The river that runs through the Nile valley descends from the tropical rain forests of central Africa. Once a year, during the summer

GRAINS ARE THE STAPLE OF LIFE

Grains were the food staples of ancient civilizations just as they are today. As long as 10,000 years ago, our ancestors gathered wild versions of wheat and other grains. Grains are actually wild grass. The edible part of the grass is the grain, which is hidden inside the florets of the wheat spikelets. Making flour from these grasses involves harvesting the grain, separating the individual spikelets, and then removing the husks and protective layers to extract the germ, the edible part. The germ is then ground into flour that is then used to make bread.

rainy season, more water flows down the river than can be held by its banks. The river then gently overflows its banks, flooding the land and depositing a black, silty soil over the valley. (Silt is a fine-grained soil, coarser than clay but finer than sand.) It is this soil, having been transported by the floodwaters from the central African highlands, that enriches the valley. However, once the floodwaters recede and the soil is baked in the sun, it can become as hard as stone and plants can't continue to grow without receiving additional water. The ancient Egyptians recognized this and also noticed that, during the floods, there was more water than they could use. So they built a system of canals or channels cut into the ground to guide the water and dikes (walls of earth) to contain the water (Figure 3.1). The canals led the water from the river to the plots where the Egyptians wanted to grow plants. In this way they could lead the water far away from the areas near the river that were normally flooded. The dikes separated the land into smaller plots that would hold the water longer, allowing the Egyptians to plant seeds in

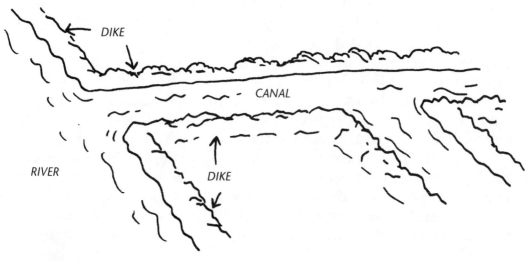

Figure 3.1

the still-moist ground. The Egyptians also built reservoirs to hold the floodwaters. They could release the water into the canals and dikes during the dry seasons, thus allowing crops to grow all year long. In the process, they learned that some soils allow water to percolate, that is, to seep through, and others are impermeable, that is, water won't seep through them.

Percolation Rate

This experiment compares the time it takes for water to pass through various types of soil.

MATERIALS
- Scissors
- 1 paper coffee filter
- Funnel
- 1 cup of sand
- Tall glass
- 10 ounces (300 ml) of water
- 1 cup of potting soil
- 1 cup of dry clay (found at art supply stores)
- Stopwatch or wristwatch with a second hand

Figure 3.2

Cut off the top of the filter so that only a 2-inch- (50-mm-) high cone remains and place this inside the funnel. Fill the funnel with the sand and place the funnel on top of the glass. Mark down the time you start pouring and then pour exactly 5 ounces (100 ml) of water into the funnel. Mark the time the water stops seeping into the glass. The percolation rate is the ounces (milliliters) of water divided by the time in minutes (oz/min [ml/min]) it takes for all the water to seep into the glass. Repeat the experiment with the potting soil and then the clay and note the differences in percolation rate (Figure 3.2).

As the Egyptian peasants began to build dikes, sluices (small water channels with a gate to control the flow of water), and canals, the irrigation system became so complicated and employed so many people that the government took control of it. Officers of the court were put in charge of the construction of the canals and waterworks. These waterworks that were so important to the ancient Egyptians are now long gone, washed away by thousands of floods and replaced with modern dams and flood-control devices. Meanwhile, the Great Pyramids that were built around the same time are still standing majestically.

In every corner of the world, different civilizations developed different ways of irrigating the land. The Incas who lived in Peru had to farm on sandy, dry soil on the coast of the Pacific Ocean. They needed fresh water to irrigate the land because salty ocean water that was nearby would have killed their crops. To bring the water from the lakes high up on the mountains, they constructed canals and underground aqueducts. These aqueducts, some of which were more than 450 miles (750 km) long, were built out of huge blocks of stone fitted closely together without any mortar to "glue" them together. Amazingly, the Incas were able to cut into the rock using only stone tools since they did not have iron (Figure 3.3).

Figure 3.3

Growing Plants in Salt Water Versus Fresh Water

MATERIALS
- Marker
- Tomato or other small greenhouse plants in individual containers
- 4 empty 1-liter plastic bottles
- Water
- 6 teaspoons salt

Using the marker, number the four plants 1, 2, 3, and 4 and do the same with the four bottles. Fill the bottles with water. In the bottle marked number 2, add one teaspoon of salt. In bottle number 3, add two teaspoons of salt, and in bottle number 4 add three teaspoons of salt. Water each of the plants with its identically marked water bottle. Be careful not to overwater the plants. Over the next few weeks, observe which plant thrives and which withers or dies, and note how the salt concentration affects the plants' health.

In Asia, where the principal crop is rice, a different irrigation technique was needed. Rice grows in fields or paddies that are filled with water. The peoples of Asia developed the concept of placing dikes around the paddies and channeling water from reservoirs to keep the rice in the paddies submerged. This technique was even used in hilly terrain where terraces were cut into the mountainsides to create giant steps, each of which was a rice paddy. In the Philippines, there are spectacular rice terraces that have existed for two thousand years, carved out of the mountainside by the Ifugao people.

Of course, there is a problem in trying to raise water to higher and higher terraces if the source of the water is at the base of the hill. Today, we have mechanical pumps to do the job, but, in earlier times, farmers relied on people and animals to carry water in buckets up hills. One of the first mechanical devices used to raise water was the water wheel, which looks like a Ferris wheel with water buckets instead of cabins (Figure 3.4). The water buckets pick up water from a stream or canal and discharge it from the top of the wheel into a higher-level canal or sluice. To turn the water wheel, farmers relied on oxen or horses that walked round and round a central post attached to a wooden arm that turned a gear connected to the water wheel.

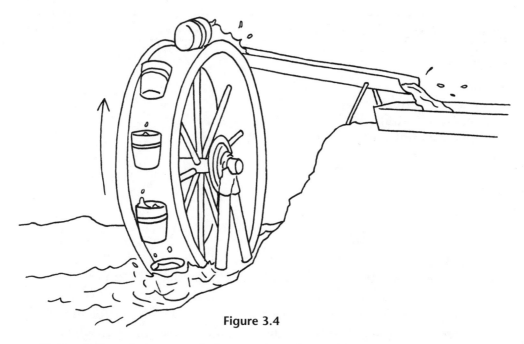

Figure 3.4

One of the cleverest of the ancient inventions to raise water was the Archimedes screw—a spiraling plate that looks like a screw and is turned inside a tube whose bottom is in the water. As the screw turns, water spirals upward and discharges at the top.

Build an Archimedes Screw

MATERIALS
- Ruler
- Cardboard tube, about 2¹/₂ inches (60 mm) in diameter and 12 inches (300 mm) long, or 1 center of a paper towel roll
- 1 sheet of thin cardboard, about 8 x 14 inches (200 x 350 mm)
- Pencil
- Protractor

- Scissors
- 1 thin dowel, about 16 inches (400 mm) long and ¹/₄ inch (6 mm) to ³/₈ inch (10 mm) in diameter
- Tape
- Stapler
- Glue
- Wire coat hanger
- Shellac or polyurethane (optional)

Use the ruler to measure the diameter of the cardboard tube. On the cardboard sheet, use a protractor with a pencil to draw six or more circles with the same diameter. Cut them out. Hold the dowel at the center of each circle and draw its circumference. Then, cut a radial (straight) line from the outside edge of each large circle to the edge of each smaller circle and cut out the smaller circles (Figure 3.5). You should now have at least six discs with holes in the middle. You will staple and tape these discs together so that they take the shape of a spiral. Place two discs on top of each other so that the radial cuts overlap slightly. Staple and tape together the area where the cardboard overlaps (Figure 3.6). Place another disc on top of these two, and join it in the same manner. Repeat this with the rest of the

Figure 3.5

discs. If you stretch out your construction, it will take the shape of a spiral. Slip it over one end of the dowel and spread the spiral along its length. Glue the inner edges of the spiral to the dowel. Squeeze the wire hanger into the form of a handle and twist it around one end of the dowel. You may have to whittle two sides of the dowel to flatten it so that the handle will not rotate (Figure 3.7).

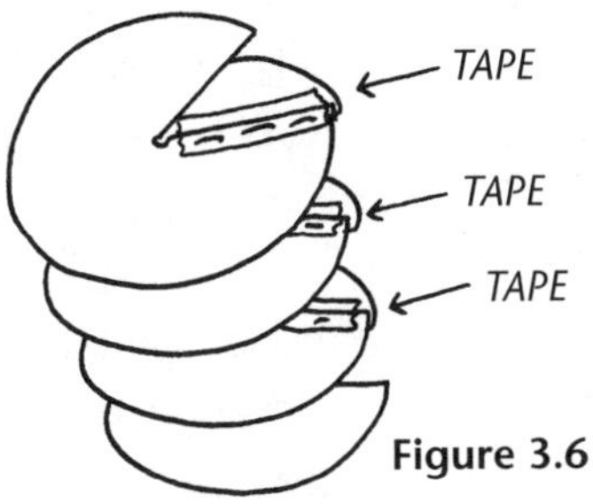

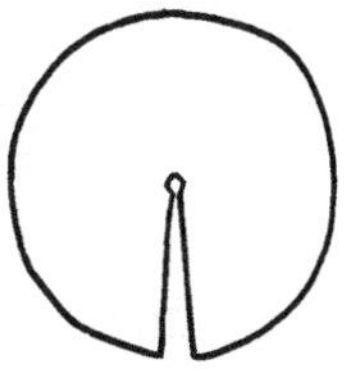

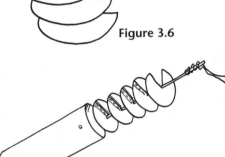

TAPE

TAPE

TAPE

Figure 3.6

Note the length of your spiral and cut a $1/4$ inch- (10-mm-) diameter hole on the side of the large tube at a point just below where the top of the spiral

Figure 3.7

will end. Place the spiral into the large tube. You now have an Archimedes screw. If you place the screw into a pan of water and turn it by the handle while holding the large tube, you will raise the water to the level of the hole. If you want your Archimedes screw to last, paint it with shellac or polyurethane.

Irrigation is as important today as it has been since the time of the ancient Egyptians. It is in fact more important today because we now have to feed a population one hundred times larger. The difference is that now the waterworks are bigger and are run by electricity and machines. Huge dams to hold water in reservoirs, such as the Aswan Dam in Egypt and the Hoover Dam in Nevada, are also used to generate electricity by channeling the great force of the stored water through turbines that run electric generators. The multi-purpose Grand Coulee Dam built on the Columbia River in Washington State supplies enough water to irrigate more than 500,000 acres (200,000 hectares) and enough power to supply most of the cities of the northwestern United States.

Finally, the canal system in California that diverts water from northern California and from the Colorado River to the Imperial Valley and southern California provides us with water to irrigate a source of winter fruits and vegetables. But there are problems. Sometimes dams break and cause flooding and death. Also, dams and canals change the natural ecology of a region, that is, how nature established a balance between wet and dry regions. When a dam is built, the reservoir behind it floods large areas of land, drowning trees and sometimes towns and villages. Of course, residents are given time to move elsewhere. This happened at the Quabbin Reservoir in Massachusetts at the beginning of the 20th century and is currently taking place at the site of the Three Gorges Dam in China. Dams also prevent fish from swimming upstream beyond the face of the dam. Fish ladders, a series of higher and higher pools, have been installed at some dams to help fix this problem. Along the Nile Valley, the construction of the Aswan Dam has changed the life of the farmers. Water no longer spreads during the annual floods but is now distributed to the farms in the valley in a controlled manner. As a consequence, the nutrients that descended from the central African highlands are now trapped behind the dam. Without these natural nutrients, the Egyptian farmers must use artificial fertilizers. These fertilizers contain elements called phosphates that poison the water into which they drain.

Now, if you are asked to design an irrigation system, we hope you will study the natural balance of the region and what your construction will do to upset it. Then, you will surely find a solution that is of benefit to humanity while at the same time respecting nature.

Infrastructure Activities

🏛 For your region of the world, draw a time schedule showing when water needs to be placed in a reservoir and when it should be released for irrigation and for navigation. In California, for instance, water needs to be stored between March and April and released between July and October.

🏛 Write a story about the Ifugao people describing how you think they built their rice paddies and how they controlled the flow of water.

🏛 Build a model of an irrigation system outdoors where you are allowed to dig. From a bucket, which represents your reservoir, pour water into one end of your system and see how it flows and distributes. Make corrections to the slopes of your channels to improve the distribution of the water. Use your imagination to make it simple or more elaborate.

4

Red, Blue, and Black Highways

The Hudson River which flows between the cities of New York and Albany, provides a natural pathway for travelers and goods. However, between Albany and Buffalo there was no such water pathway until the Erie Canal was built allowing boats to complete the journey. But, there are only a limited number of rivers and even fewer canals in the world. So roads were developed to travel across land. At first there were footpaths and horsepaths that later became cartpaths as horses were used to pull carts and wagons. The first roads were just trampled-down paths that became muddy whenever it rained. To overcome this messy condition, ancient civilizations decided to pave their most important and most highly traveled roads.

All Roads Lead to Rome

The Romans were the greatest of the ancient road builders because they needed good roads to connect the cities of their vast empire. Since they believed that their empire would last forever, the Romans were careful to build roads that would last and not be washed or worn away. To achieve this, they built their roads of many layers, each of which fulfilled a special function. They first excavated the topsoil to reach a base that was generally dry natural soil. Sometimes this base was mixed with broken stones and shaped to provide drainage away from the center of the road. A middle layer of gravel and sand gave the road its strength. The top layer was pavement that could be repaired as it became worn down by carts and horses' hooves. This layer was composed of either stone slabs or tamped gravel or flint, depending on the road's importance (Figure 4.1). Therefore, the surface of the road was above the level of the ground on either side and was called a highway. On either side of these roads were ditches to carry away rainwater. Successive Roman emperors built more than 50,000 miles (80,000 km) of roads, some of which are still in use. Portions of the Appian Way, which leads from Rome to Brindisi on the heel (southwest coast) of Italy, can still be seen today with ruts in the stone pavers where Roman chariots wore down the stone 2,000 years ago.

TOP LAYER OF STONE

MIDDLE LAYER OF GRAVEL AND SAND

BASE LAYER OF BROKEN STONES

Figure 4.1

Interestingly, Roman roads were built in absolutely straight lines. If there was a hill in the way, the road went straight up the hill and straight down the other side. These hill roads could become very steep. Apart from the simplicity of building straight roads, going from one hilltop to another had another purpose. Just like Native Americans, the Roman army used smoke signals to communicate. Since the roads were built primarily for armies, signal stations were erected at the top of each hill. These stations were 80-foot- (25-m-) high towers topped with cauldrons of burning oil. Soldiers could use these cauldrons to pass along a message to the next hill by waving a cloth over the smoky fire. In this way news from the outer reaches of the empire was transmitted back to Rome in a day. This was pretty quick, considering that traveling the same distance could take weeks.

Build a Groma

Try your hand at making a groma, or a Roman surveyor's tool. This device helped the Romans build straight roads.

MATERIALS
- **Craft knife**
- **Dowel, about 3¼ feet (1m) long and ³/₈ inch (10 mm) in diameter**
- **4 equal weights, or 4 of the same beads or washers**
- **4 pieces of string, each about 2 feet (600 mm) long and ¼ inch (6 mm) in diameter**
- **2 dowels, each about 1 foot (300 mm) long**
- **Super glue**

ADULT SUPERVISION RECOMMENDED.

Have an adult use the knife to whittle the end of the 3¼ foot- (1 m-) long dowel into a point. Tie a bead or washer to one end of each piece of

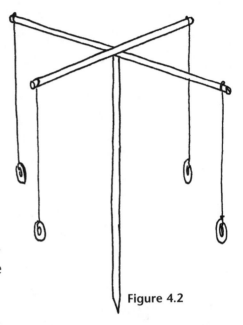

Figure 4.2

string. Mark the center of the two shorter dowels and glue them together at the center so that they are perpendicular to each other (the dowels should form a cross). Be careful not to get any super glue on your fingers. Let the glue dry completely. Next, glue the cross to the top of the long dowel by placing the cross on a table and holding the longer dowel in place upright until the glue hardens. Tie one of the strings to each of the four ends of the cross. You have built a groma (Figure 4.2).

To see how the groma works, take it outside and plant the pointy end down in the ground. Make sure that the stake, or the long dowel, is perfectly upright. Look at it by lying on the ground and checking if the strings are parallel to the stake. Make small adjustments by pushing the bottom of the stick sideways, taking care not to break it. Now look or sight along two strings until they are perfectly aligned and ask a friend to place stakes or sticks along that line some distance from where you are. This is how the Romans plotted perfectly straight roads.

Long before the Romans were building their empire and their road network, China had a system of roads that was divided into five classes: pathways for people and animals, narrow roads for small carts, wagon roads, two-lane wagon roads, and even a three-lane highway that allowed one wagon to pass another. This rigid organization extended even to standardizing the sizes of the wagons that were allowed and setting rules for behavior at a road crossing. Of course, speeding was strictly forbidden.

Meanwhile, in the western world after the Roman Empire fell apart between the fourth and fifth centuries A.D., there was no organization left to take care of the roads. Throughout the old empire, from England to Turkey, roads were neglected and began to crumble when people took the paving stones to build houses and fortifications. Without maintenance, many of the elegant Roman bridges that were part of the road network collapsed into the rivers or valleys below. Anyway, it was no longer safe to travel long distances since highwaymen could be expected to rob or even kill people. These were the Dark Ages in Europe.

As the western world came out of that terrible time, roads were again important as a means of communication between cities and countries. Goods needed to be transported from where they were made to where they were needed. In England, the king declared that people were to be protected along certain important roads. Religious orders took up the task of maintaining roads between centers of religious importance. Some roads in England and France were paved to allow horse-drawn wagons carrying goods to travel faster.

Roads were built between existing cities and also to reach the far away boundaries of countries. In the mid-19th-century United States, the Oregon Trail connected the settled Midwest to the new territories of Oregon and California. In this way, new towns and cities were settled as the population migrated westward.

Comparing Friction

Why is it possible to travel faster on a paved road than on a dirt road? You may answer quite rightly that a paved road is smoother than a dirt road. But how do you measure smoothness in scientific terms? Smoothness is defined by *friction*. The smoother a surface is, the less friction it has. Have you ever tried to skateboard or rollerblade on a bumpy sidewalk and found it much easier to go fast on a paved surface like a driveway or parking lot? Of course, you must be careful of cars on these surfaces.

You can compare the friction offered by different road surfaces with the following experiment.

MATERIALS

- **1 piece of cardboard, about 18 inches (500 mm) long and 12 inches wide (300 mm)**
- **White craft glue**
- **Sand or several sheets of coarse sandpaper**
- **Assorted size wooden blocks**
- **1 small, slightly heavy, metal toy car such as a Matchbox or Hot Wheels**

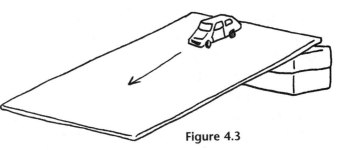

Figure 4.3

Spread white glue on one side of the cardboard and, before it dries, sprinkle sand all over the surface. Alternatively, you can glue sheets of coarse sandpaper to cover the cardboard surface. Next, place the cardboard on the floor with the clean, smooth side up and place one block under one end of the cardboard so that it slopes (Figure 4.3). See if the car will roll down the slope. If not, keep adding blocks to increase the slope of your "road" until the car rolls downhill. Repeat the experiment with the sandy or rough side up and notice how much steeper the slope has to be before the car will roll downhill. For the mathematically inclined, you can express your results as percentage friction. You take the height of the blocks divided by one hundred times the length of your slope, which gives you the frictional resistance of the surface as percent units.

Many roads were built by individual states or as private money-making ventures. In order to collect a toll or fee, a pole acting as a gate was placed across these roads every few miles or kilometers. This pole, also called a pike, was turned aside to let the traveler pass once he had paid the toll to the toll keeper. Consequently, these roads were called turnpikes and were the predecessors of today's turnpikes.

Until the industrial revolution in the middle of the 19th century, other parts of the world never had roads to equal those built 2,000 years ago by the Romans. But the real push to build roads came with the invention of the automobile at the turn of the 20th century.

Automobiles

Early automobiles were carriages on which engines were mounted. The first was a steam engine-driven, three-wheeled vehicle invented by a French engineer, Nicolas J. Cugnot in 1789. In the late 19th century, the internal combustion engine was developed, in which a fuel (gasoline) is fed into a cylinder and ignited. The explosion causes an expansion of the gases in the cylinder and pushes the piston as in a steam engine (Figure 5.6 on page 53). Inventors in many countries developed practical engines and cars, but the most practical was invented by Gottlieb Daimler in 1885. The Duryea brothers were the first to manufacture and sell cars in the United States, but Henry Ford popularized the automobile by mass producing the vehicles in a factory. However, steam-driven cars were popular until 1920. The world was not prepared for the introduction of the automobile, and roads were at first unable to handle this new means of transportation.

In 1909, Alice Ramsey decided to drive across the United States in one of the early automobiles. She declared, "I see no reason why any woman who can drive a car cannot take one across the continent." Together with three friends, she set out on a 3,700-mile (6,000-km) trip from New York to San Francisco in an open, 30 hp Maxwell car. It took them almost two months, which is not surprising considering the difficulties they had to overcome. First, there were no maps to follow so they had to navigate by driving to the tops of hills and looking for telephone wires that would identify the transcontinental railroad, which they were following. Generally, telephone wires followed the same path that the railroads did. Second, there were no gas stations, so they had to carry extra gas cans and obtain gas wherever there were storage yards. Furthermore, there were no paved roads, so the party followed horsepaths where they existed and even crossed open fields where no path could be found. Whenever it rained, the paths turned soupy and the car would often get stuck, needing to be pulled out by horses provided by local farmers (who would charge the ladies for their services). Sometimes they would follow the railroad tracks and end up bumping along the track to cross a bridge when there were no bridges for cars. All along the way they had many adventures and many mechanical problems. An axle broke when they hit a deep hole in the road and the tie rod that held the front wheels broke when a bolt holding it to one of the wheels fell out. This caused the wheels to splay out and the car to fall flat on the ground. Fortunately, there were friendly ranches along the way with iron forges, usually used to make horseshoes. The forges could just as well repair the car's broken parts. Of course, the travelers had numerous flat tires along the way. They carried a supply of inner tubes to replace the ones that burst. Trips like this one demonstrated the need for better roads between cities and the need to plan the road network as part of an urban regional plan.

Compare this story to today's transcontinental driver, who can complete the same journey in less than a week, driving along superhighways and resting at night in motels. In the United States, the interstate highway system is still only slightly more than half as long as roads of the Roman Empire. Open a map of the United States and look at the maze of roads that crisscross every corner of the country. You will see the red highways, which are the superhighways with numerous lanes in each direction. Then there are the blue highways, which are four-lane roads connecting many cities. Finally, there are the black highways, which are two-lane country roads. On some maps you may even see dashed black lines, which are dirt roads that may not be passable in all seasons. All these roads allow us to move easily from one place to another, more easily than at any time in history, except within the city. In 1900, when there were only 10,000 cars in the world, the average speed of cars within the city was 8 miles per hour (13 km/hr). Today, when there are 600 million cars in the world, they move around the city at an average of only 11 miles per hour (18 km/hr). Not much of an improvement! Sometimes drivers are so anxious to cross an intersection that they get caught in the middle and prevent traffic from moving in the other direction. This causes "gridlock," with cars stopped in all directions.

One of the consequences of the car was the spread of the city into surrounding green areas. The car and the network of roads built also resulted in new towns and villages that were no longer tied to rivers. It also allowed people to move farther from where they worked and consequently led to the growth of suburbs.

Airports

People have always been fascinated by the idea of flying. Greek mythology tells the story of Icarus, a young man who wanted so much to fly that he put on a pair of wings made of wax. Unfortunately, as he flew up into the sunny morning, his waxen wings began to melt from the heat of the sun and Icarus plunged to Earth. Many people tried to imitate birds, but none succeeded until bicycle makers Wilbur and Orville Wright built and flew the first airplane in 1903. The small and light early airplanes needed only a grass field for takeoff and landing. As planes became larger and more powerful, specially built landing fields were needed, leading to the development of *airfields*. Essentially, airports were short sections of paved road that permitted the airplanes to land and take off while the rest of the journey took place along airways in the sky. Within 30 years after the invention of the airplane, every city and town had to have at least one airport to satisfy a growing need for more landing spaces. Today, a part of any city's infrastructure is its airports.

Infrastructure Activities

ADULT SUPERVISION RECOMMENDED.

With a friend, stand at the side of the road and perform a traffic count. To do this, count the number of cars and trucks that pass your location in 15-minute segments. Do this at various times of the day. Construct a graph on which you plot the number of cars and the number of trucks at various times. You will notice that there is more traffic at certain times of the day. Why?

On a map, locate a city or town in another part of your country. Plot the roads you would need to reach the far-off town and how many miles would need to be driven. Now plot a straight line between your town and the far-off town and measure the distance. This is the path that an airplane would take. Is the airplane route shorter than the automobile route? By guessing how fast you can drive and how fast you can fly, calculate how long the car trip and airplane trip would take.

5
The Iron Horse

Rivers and canals provided the best way to transport goods over long distances until the middle of the 19th century, when the railroad came into popular use. In the late 18th century in Europe, the companies that controlled the canals began to treat their customers badly by slowing the movement of goods. For instance, it took less time for cotton to arrive at the dock in Liverpool, England, from New York City than it took to travel one-tenth the distance through a canal from Liverpool to Manchester. The frustrated mill owners wanted to find another way to ship their cotton. They turned to George Stephenson, who had invented a steam locomotive. Stephenson had seen railways used in coal mines where horses pulled cars that rode on iron rails. Stephenson thought that a steam locomotive could replace the horses. He was right. Thereafter, his locomotive was known as the *iron horse*.

However, railways were not a new idea. They were first used 400 years ago to transport coal in England. Of course, these early railways were different from the ones we know today. The rails were wood planks resting on wood sleepers, which were similar to the wood or concrete ties that support today's steel rails. Nailed to the rail was a half-round oak molding on which the pulleylike wheels of the rail cars rode (Figure 5.1). These oak moldings wore out quickly. In 1740, longer-lasting iron moldings were invented and they replaced the oak

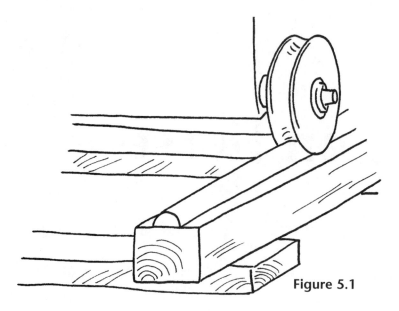

Figure 5.1

moldings. Later the rail-wheel assembly was changed to the flanged wheel and cast-edge rail that are used today (Figure 5.2).

Figure 5.2

When the mill owners approached Stephenson in 1828, he offered to build a 30-mile- (48-km-) long railway between Liverpool and Manchester. He decided that a railway should run practically level, which meant that he would have to build a tunnel between the two cities, cut down a rocky hill, and cross a bog. Although he was a great engineer, he didn't know much about construction, so all these problems greatly increased the cost of the railway. He needed to borrow a great deal of money to finish the job. Before being given the money, a contest was held to choose the engine for the train. The winning engine was the "Rocket," designed and built by Stephenson's 20-year-old son, Robert. This locomotive was capable of pulling three times its own weight at a speed of 12.5 mph (20 km/hr), about the same speed as that attained by an Olympic long-distance runner. When hauling lighter passenger cars, it achieved the fabulous speed of 24 mph (39 km/hr). Although the line was more expensive than anyone expected, it was a great success, and it led to railroads being built all over the world.

Build a Level

MATERIALS
- **Test tube with a cork or rubber stopper**
- **Baby oil**

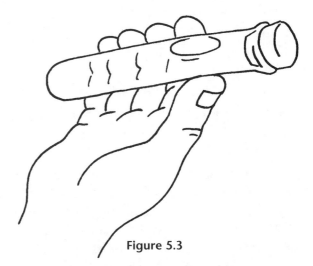

Figure 5.3

Partially fill the test tube with baby oil so that only a small space remains between the top of the oil and the stopper. Close the tube tightly and hold it almost horizontally. Notice that a bubble moves back and forth as you wiggle the tube (Figure 5.3). When the bubble is exactly in the center of the length of the tube, it is horizontal and you have a level.

Stephenson was only partly right when he decided that a railroad should travel on a horizontal track. Because both the tracks and the wheels are made of smooth steel, it is understandable that he should conclude that the wheel would slide on a sloped track. But even smooth steel is not totally slippery. If you were to look at the surface with a magnifying glass, you would see many ridges and bumps. These ridges and bumps cause friction when you try to slide one piece of steel over another.

Friction

The smoother the road surface, the less the frictional resistance. But what is friction and what does it depend upon?

MATERIALS
- **1 piece of wood, at least 8 inches (200 mm) on each side**
- **Drill**
- **String**
- **Spring scale (similar to the one used to weigh vegetables at the store)**
- **Bathroom scale**
- **Cooking pot, 4 quart (4 l) capacity**

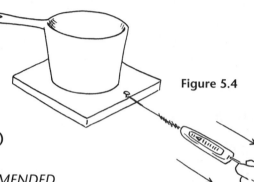

Figure 5.4

ADULT SUPERVISION RECOMMENDED.

Have an adult drill a hole in the middle of one side of the wood, about 1 inch from the edge. The hole should be large enough so that the string will fit through it.

Attach the spring scale to the edge of the wood plank with a string so that you can pull it along the floor. Weigh the pot and plank together on the bathroom scale and record the weight. Place the pot on the plank (Figure 5.4) and pull the end of the spring scale slowly but steadily. Note that the indicator on the scale first goes up and then settles down to a constant value for the pulling force. This happens because there is an initial friction that keeps the board from moving that is larger than the force you need to move it steadily. Record the value of the steady pulling force. Now fill the pot half full of water and weigh the pot and the plank on the bathroom scale. Pull the spring scale and record the value. Repeat the experiment again, this time with a full pot of water.

Prepare a table and record your results in the following form.

	Weight	Pulling force	Friction (pulling force / weight)
Empty pot			
Half full pot			
Full pot			

The numbers in the last column are obtained by dividing the pulling force by the weight, a dimensionless number. You will notice that this number is essentially the same for all three cases you tested. This is the friction factor. If you were to repeat the experiment using steel sliding against steel or wood against steel, you would note that the friction factor depends on the materials that slide against each other. As the "Comparing Friction" experiment in chapter four demonstrated, the smoother a surface is, the less friction it has.

You can also conclude from the experiment that the larger the pulling force, the heavier the weight of the object to be moved. But of course you knew that, because at home you can push a chair more easily than the living room couch.

Because of friction, a train does not have to travel on a perfectly horizontal track but can climb a gradient (the ratio of the vertical rise to the horizontal distance) of 1 to 11. Any steeper and the train will slide backward. This limitation is not important in the relatively flat central United States. But crossing the Appalachian or Rocky Mountains, or mountains anywhere in the world, requires that tunnels be bored through the mountains or shelves cut on the mountainsides to maintain small enough gradients.

Because they were practical and efficient, railroads were built at a rapid pace throughout the world. Travel by railroad cars riding on smooth iron rails was much more comfortable than travel by stagecoach on bumpy roads. Consequently, thousands of miles of new rails were laid every year after 1830, and by the end of the century the United States had over 190,000 miles (300,000 kilometers) of track. Perhaps the most spectacular achievement of the early railroad pioneers was the construction of the transcontinental railroad.

The Transcontinental Railroad

Early American pioneers who traveled from St. Louis, Missouri, to California, Oregon, and Washington took from four to six months to complete the trip. It was an incredibly difficult and slow journey that included crossing scorched deserts and frozen mountains using wagons laboriously pulled by oxen. There had to be a better way. By mid-century, the railroad was well established in the eastern United States, with branches going in all directions. Also by that time, the amount of freight hauled by wagons going east from California was rapidly increasing. It was time to join the two parts of the country separated by the Rocky Mountain chain. The Transcontinental Railroad would reduce travel time between the eastern and western United States

STANDARD GAUGE

Figure 5.5

The gauge of a railroad is the distance between the rails. When George Stephenson built the Liverpool-Manchester line, he used the same gauge that had been used for the coal mine trams, which was 4 feet, 8½ inches (1,435 mm). Legend has it that this was the exact distance between the wheels of imperial Roman chariots, which were made just wide enough to accommodate the back ends of two war horses. Early English stagecoaches had been built to fit in the grooves worn down by chariot wheels in the roads built by the ancient Romans. This is the *standard gauge* for railroads throughout most of the world. But it wasn't always so. In the late 19th century the United States had 23 different gauges, from 3 feet (1 m) to almost 10 feet (3 m). Even today there are places in the world where other gauges are used. Russia, Spain, and parts of South America still have gauges larger than the standard gauge, and mountain railroads like those in Switzerland use a narrower gauge. The narrow-gauge trains are smaller and can go around sharper curves, making them practical on curvy mountainsides (Figure 5.5).

from six months to six days. President Abraham Lincoln signed an act to authorize construction of a transcontinental railway on July 1, 1862. Similar to the method Eupalinus, the Greek engineer mentioned in chapter one, used for building his aqueduct, the railroad was built from both ends in order to save time. Two companies, one moving east from California and one moving west from Nebraska, began to construct the pathway and lay track. Since the two companies were promised a cash bonus that depended on how much track was laid, a furious competition ensued. Explorers, surveyors, trestle and bridge builders, tunnel blasters, and spikers (the men who drove the spikes that held the rails to the wooden cross-ties) worked at a mad pace to advance the construction. Because the act of Congress calling for the Transcontinental Railroad did not specify where—or even if—the crews should meet, for several miles parallel tracks were

STANDARD TIME

Until the expansion of railroads, clocks were always set based on the position of the sun. When the sun was directly overhead, clocks in that location were set to noon. Since every town set time in this manner, if it was 12:00 in Chicago, Illinois, it was 12:31 in Pittsburgh, Pennsylvania, and 11:50 in St. Louis, Missouri (remember, the sun moves from east to west so it is always earlier in the west than in the east). Consequently, in the 19th century, there were more than 100 different time standards used by American railroads, which created tremendous confusion. In 1883, Standard Time was adopted and the time zones were established. Standard Time resulted in creating only four time zones for the continental United States; each zone was separated by exactly one hour, and this system greatly simplified railroad timetables.

built in Utah until Congress decided where the rail lines should meet. Finally, on May 10, 1869, the two crews met at Promontory, Utah, and there was a huge celebration as the last rail was attached to the wooden tie with a golden spike.

Steam Engine

Of course, rail travel was made possible by the development of the steam locomotive. This is essentially a steam engine on wheels. Inside the engine, a fire, fed by wood or coal, burns in a fire box that is used to heat water in a looped pipe. As the water boils, steam is produced that cannot escape the pipe and therefore pushes, or creates *pressure*, against the sides of the pipe. When the pressure is high enough, a

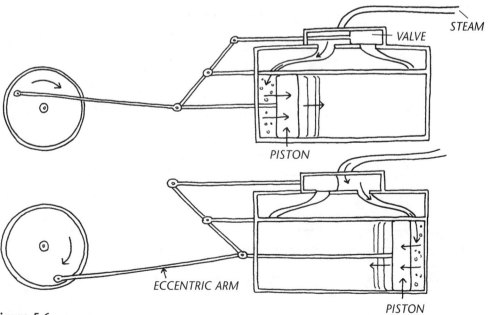

Figure 5.6

valve opens at the end of the pipe and the steam flows into a cylinder in which there is a piston. The steam pushes the piston, which is connected by a rod pinned to a rotating wheel. When the piston reaches the end of the cylinder, the first valve closes and a second one opens up to let the steam enter at the other end of the piston, pushing it back. The back-and-forth motion of the piston in the cylinder is transformed by the rod (connected to a point away from the wheel's axis) into a rotating movement of the wheel that then drives the steam locomotive (Figure 5.6). Unfortunately, the fire used to heat the water created a dusty, black smoke that was not welcomed in the cities. Consequently, most train stations were located near the edge of the cities and were covered to protect passengers from rain and snow but open to let the smoke escape.

Some trains, however, were used in the center of the cities.

Trams

City trains that ran on iron tracks that were set down into the streets were called tramways. The earliest ones were pulled by horses, like the horse-drawn coaches that preceded them. In 1872, a flu epidemic struck the horses that were used to pull trams in New York City, killing more than 20,000 of them. To avoid a similar tragedy and expense, steam locomotives were tried as a replacement. To the great joy of everyone who lived near a tramway, the noisy, dirty, and smoky steam locomotives were soon replaced by electric trams (or trolley cars).

Figure 5.7

WHAT IS A CATENARY?

Take a rope or chain of any length and hold one end in each hand. Let the rope or chain hang loosely between your hands. The shape taken by the rope or cable under only its own weight is called a catenary (after the Latin word *catena*, or chain). If you were to freeze the shape and trace its contours on a piece of paper and draw a circle with the same end points and the same

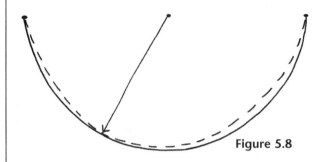

bottom point (Figure 5.8), you would notice that the catenary lies inside the circle.

The reason the electric wire that feeds the electric train is called a catenary is that the curved wire that holds the horizontal wire has (almost) the shape of a catenary.

Figure 5.8

Other ways of moving rail cars were also introduced. One such system was the cable car, which was introduced in San Francisco in 1873. There is no motor in a cable car. Instead, a continuous cable runs under the street to a plant where a big motor keeps the cable moving at a constant speed. The cable car has a gripper that slips into a slot in the road. The gripper grabs the cable to get the car moving and releases it to stop the car (Figure 5.7). Of course, there is also a brake to stop the wheels and keep the car from sliding.

Electric trams, some with overhead *catenary* cables for power and some with power lines on or under roads, were also built in most cities in the late 19th century. They remained the main city transportation vehicles until the second half of the 20th century, when most trams were replaced by buses. Today, many new electric trains are being built in cities; but, to make them seem like a more modern invention, they are called *light rail* systems.

In densely populated cities such as Paris, London, and New York City, city railroads were built underground and called subways, metros, or simply the underground. Some of these railroads were built by digging a trench, constructing the box into which the subway would run, and then covering the box with earth. This is still called the *cut and cover* method of building a tunnel. Others tunnels were bored using a machine to drill horizontally into the earth or rock.

Cut and Cover

This experiment is best done at the beach or in a backyard where you are allowed to dig.

MATERIALS
- **1 6 x 14 inch (150 mm x 350 mm) sheet of cardboard**
- **Tape**
- **Hand trowel, or small shovel or cup to scoop dirt**
- **1 center of a paper towel roll**

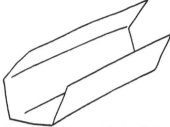

Figure 5.9

Make a square tube out of a sheet of cardboard. Fold the long side of the cardboard in half and fold each half in half again in the long direction (Figure 5.9). Create your square tube by folding the bent edges into a tubular form and then taping the open edges together. You should now have two tubes, the round paper towel roll and the square tube you have just made.

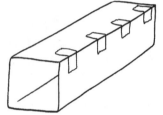

At the beach or in the yard, dig two trenches, each about 5 inches (130 mm) deep and the length of each of the tubes. Slope the ends of each trench up to meet the ground surface. Place each of the tubes in one of the trenches and cover with sand or soil. Make certain you have at least 3 inches (80 mm) of sand above the top of the tubes. Tamp the sand to make certain that it fills all the area around the tubes. Look in from the end to see your tunnel. Note the shape of each. Next, walk on top of your tunnels or press the soil down. Look again from the tunnel ends and see what has happened to the shape of each of these tunnels. Which shape seems to be the strongest?

Tunnels are not just for subways. In Switzerland and other mountainous regions of the world, tunnels had to be bored through mountains to keep the grade of the railroads (and the roads) low. Tunnels were also bored for waterlines. At first, the construction of tunnels was laborious, using hand tools such as picks and hand drills. With such tools, a day's progress was measured in inches. In the late 19th century, the introduction of drills operated by compressed air and later compressed water greatly speeded up the operation. By the beginning of the 20th century, electrically driven drills mounted on big racks cut through the face of rock faster, advancing construction by feet (meters) instead of inches (millimeters) per day. Other types of machines were developed to push a tunnel through soft rock or earth. This method was used to construct one of the most spectacular of modern tunnels, the "Chunnel" under the English Channel.

The Chunnel

England and France are separated by a section of the North Atlantic Ocean that narrows to as little as 21 miles (34 km) and is called *La Manche*, or "the sleeve" in French. For the longest time, passengers who wanted to travel from London, England, to Paris, France, had to take a train to a city on the channel coast, such as Dover. Once they arrived at the coast, they would transfer to a ferry that took them to the French coast. When they arrived in France, they would have to board another train to take them to Paris. Looking at a map, it is easy to see what a difficult trip this was. A very long time ago (more than 11,000 years), before the end of the last Ice Age, these same travelers could have walked across the channel—it was covered with a thick layer of ice.

In the past, there was no reason to make the passage between France and England easy because for centuries the two countries had been enemies. It was only in the late 19th century that they became uneasy allies. One of the first ideas for a link between the two countries was a scheme for a tunnel in which horse-drawn coaches would safely carry passengers under the raging sea. It was an impractical idea when proposed by Albert Favier in 1802, since no one had ever built a tunnel under water before. In 1880, the construction of a tunnel was actually started but was stopped by the English Parliament because they thought it could lead to an invasion of their country. A century later, after many other false starts, construction of the tunnel finally began in 1987. Starting from both the English and the French coasts, huge, tunnel-boring machines started digging the tunnels. There are actually three: two traffic tunnels and a small service tunnel. Precast concrete rings to line the tunnels were installed behind the forward-moving machines. Seven years later the historic link was completed and the first train, with the queen of England and the president of France aboard, crossed the channel. The trip from London to Paris could now be completed in three hours at speeds up to 185 miles per hour (300 km/hr). It was the most spectacular infrastructure project of the 20th century.

Other Trains

In some cities choked with coach traffic, trains often ran on tracks elevated above the street. Many still exist today. In Chicago, for instance, you can still ride the elevated line that loops around downtown, while in New York City most elevated lines are in the outer boroughs and were replaced by subways in the city center. The most recent elevated lines are monorails, carlike vehicles that either ride on top of a single steel or concrete guideway such as the one in Seattle, Washington, or hang from the guideway such as the one in Memphis, Tennessee (Figure 5.10).

There are places in the world with very steep hills that require a railroad, but, as we have learned, a regular railroad cannot climb a steep slope. Two inventions solved this problem: the funicular and cog railways. In a funicular, two cars riding on regular rails are attached to a cable that is looped around a big, motor-driven wheel at the top of the hill. Since a single cable joins the two cars, when one car is going up, the other goes down.

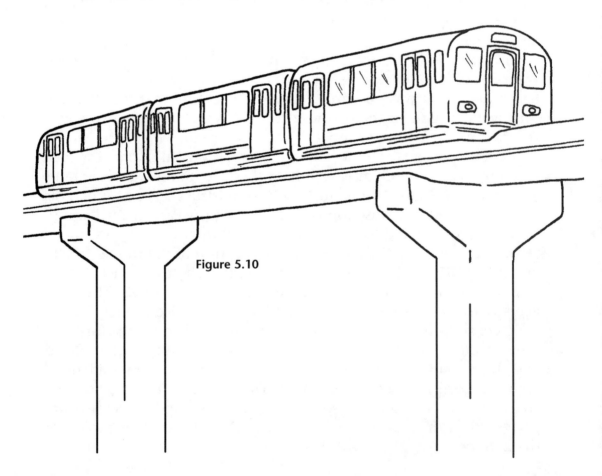

Figure 5.10

Build a Funicular

MATERIALS
- Hammer
- Nail or screw
- Twine, kite string, or carpet thread
- 2 small toy cars, such as Matchbox or Hot Wheels
- Small pulley (similar to the one used to hold down the cord of a window drapery or curtain, available at hardware or fabric stores)
- 1 plank of wood at least 16 inches (400 mm) long

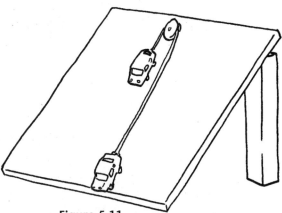
Figure 5.11

Attach the pulley to one end of the wood plank with a nail or screw. String the thread through the pulley and attach it to one of the cars that you have placed at the bottom of the wood plank. Cut the other end of the string near the pulley to attach the other car. The two cars should now be placed so that one is at the top of the plank and the other at the bottom. Tilt the plank and support it so that it stands alone. Now pull the upper car down to the bottom of the plank and watch the other car climb the hill (Figure 5.11).

Another way of moving a train up a steep hill is the cog railroad, such as the one that was built in 1869 on Mt. Washington, the highest mountain on the East Coast of the United States. This train also rides on rails but is driven by a motor in the engine that turns a cog, which is a toothed wheel. The cogwheel engages a rack, a toothed strip of steel, which is attached to the ground (Figure 5.12). The Mt.

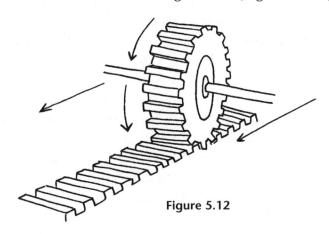
Figure 5.12

Washington train climbs an impressive 3,700 feet (1,128 m) in a distance of 3 miles (4.8 km)—an average grade of 3,700/15.840 = 24 percent). To keep the passengers comfortable, the cars are tilted so that the passenger cabin is horizontal and, as the engine is horizontal as well, we suppose it keeps the engine comfortable, too (Figure 5.13).

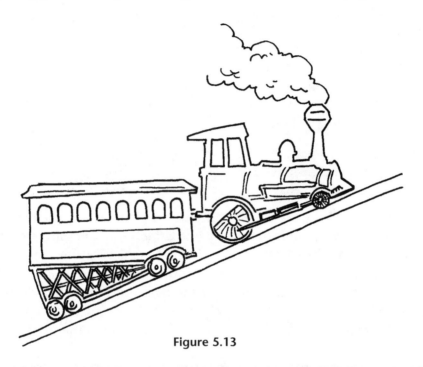

Figure 5.13

Rails used to be laid in sections about 50 feet (15 m) long. There were several reasons for this. First, it was the maximum practical length that could be handled by a crew of men. Second, steel expands and contracts as the temperature changes so that longer track sections could pull a track out of alignment as they expanded in the summer sun. This is why, when a train runs over a track, you can hear a click-clack sound as the wheel passes over the joint between the two track sections. Today, the click-clack sound has almost disappeared because engineers have learned how to smoothly join two tracks by welding and to firmly hold down the track so that it does not move around due to the sun's heat.

Train travel was so popular by the mid-19th century that 75 percent of intercity travel was by rail. Now, most people drive or fly; but, to get more of us to use safe and clean trains, new high-speed railroads are being built all over the world. The first railroad built over 150 years ago crept along at 24 mph (40 km/hr), while today's high-

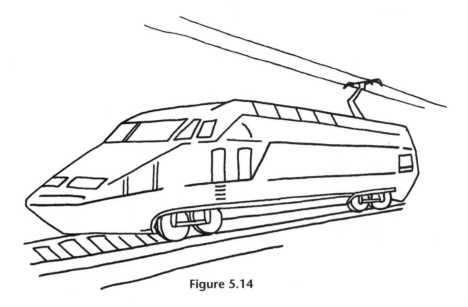

Figure 5.14

speed trains attain speeds of 250 mph (400 km/hr), and the future is open to achieve even higher speeds (Figure 5.14). Some of these fast trains don't even ride on rails but float less than an inch above a guideway. These are *maglev* or magnetic levitation trains, which use the repelling force of magnets to raise the train above the guideway. Electromagnetism also provides the means of propulsion to rapidly move the trains at speeds approaching those of airplanes.

Infrastructure Activities

🏛 Draw a pie chart showing what part of each of the following transportation systems you believe contributes to moving people and goods: Boats, barges, trains, cars, trucks, and airplanes.

🏛 Develop an idea for a fast train. Consider the shape of the train and the type of track to be used.

🏛 How fast do trains travel? On a map, measure the distance between two cities serviced by a train. Obtain a copy of a train schedule and note the time in minutes that it takes for the train to travel between the two cities. Divide the time by 60 to obtain the time in hours. Divide the distance by the time and you obtain the average speed of the train.

6
Why Do Bridges Come in So Many Shapes?

A traveler in ancient times encountering a stream faced the problem of how to cross it. Since there were trees in the woods nearby, he looked for one that was longer than the stream was wide. Then he cut down the tree, trimmed it of branches, and dropped it across the stream. Thus, what he had built was a bridge, a shaky one, that he walked across by balancing himself very carefully.

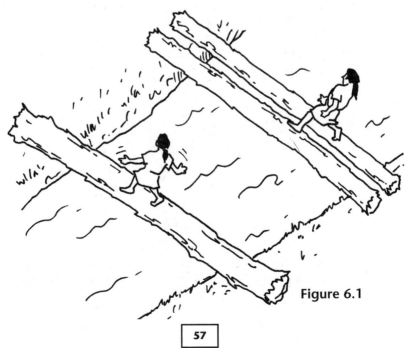

Figure 6.1

Undoubtedly he soon found out that by cutting down a second tree and putting it next to the first one, his bridge became more stable and easier to walk across (Figure 6.1).

Beam Bridges

The tree trunk used by this ancient traveler to cross a stream is called a *beam*, the simplest form of bridge. By putting two or more beams together, the resulting bridge can accommodate more than one traveler and, if made wide enough, can even permit a cart pulled by horse or oxen to cross. A beam carries a load by bending. You can observe bending by placing a pencil between two books lying on a table (just like the ancient traveler's tree trunk). As you push down the center of the pencil, note how it bends and tries to curve (Figure 6.2).

Figure 6.2

Wood was not the only material used by early bridge builders. One of the oldest bridges still standing is a stone bridge only eight feet (2.4 m) long that crosses a country stream in Portugal. Instead of wood poles, this bridge used stone slabs placed next to each other, making it a multibeam bridge. It has been estimated that it was built about 2,600 years ago.

Today, bridges using beams are built to carry both roads and railroads over short- to medium-length spans. The very short ones may use rectangular wooden beams and a wooden deck (Figure 6.3). Longer ones can be made of either steel or concrete beams with a concrete deck. These concrete or steel beams are often shaped like an *I* (Figure 6.4). Can you guess why?

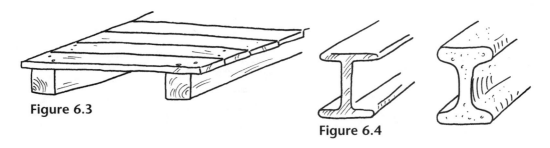

Figure 6.3

Figure 6.4

How Does a Beam Carry Loads?

MATERIALS
- **1 block of foam rubber, about 1 foot (300 mm) long, 2 inches (50 mm) wide, and 2 inches (50 mm) high**
- **Marker**
- **2 books**

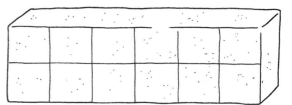

Figure 6.5

On the long side of the foam rubber block, use a marker to draw vertical lines about 2 inches (50 mm) apart and a horizontal line along the center (Figure 6.5). Place this beam so that each end rests on a book. Push down the center of the beam and observe how the lines deform. The top edge seems to have become shorter because the vertical lines are closer together at the top (Figure 6.6). The bottom edge seems to have elongated

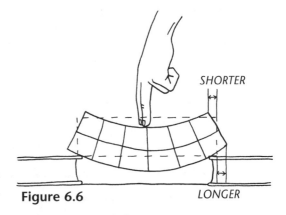

SHORTER

Figure 6.6   LONGER

because the vertical lines are farther apart at the bottom. The long middle line does not appear to have changed length.

Since it stretched, the edge that lengthened is in *tension* while the edge that shortened is in *compression*. The center of the beam has neither tension nor compression so you can conclude that starting from the middle, the closer to the top, the more the compression. In the same way, moving down from the center, the tension increases toward the bottom. This means that the beam's bending strength is greatest at the top and bottom and the center can be carved away since it is not contributing much to its bending strength. That is the reason many beams are in the shape of an *I*.

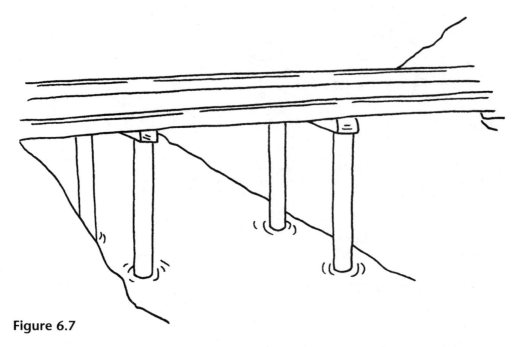

Figure 6.7

Bridges using trees were limited by the height of the trunk. Also, since tree trunks taper to smaller diameters at the top, only the fatter, lower parts of the tree could be used as a bridge. This meant that you could not build long bridges unless you placed piers in the river or valley to keep the span short (Figure 6.7). Trestles, popular in the

Figure 6.8

western United States in the 19th century, were assembled for short-span bridges using available lumber (Figure 6.8). In the same way, building bridges out of stone slabs was limited by the size of the stones that could be quarried and moved to the bridge site. To build bridges with longer spans required an innovative idea, for which we have the Romans to thank.

Arch Bridges

The Romans, as we have already shown in chapter 4, were master road builders as well as builders of great aqueducts. As they advanced their roads and aqueducts, they were faced with the problem of crossing large rivers and deep valleys. Wood or stone beams could not span these great distances so they developed a unique building form: the *arch*.

An arch is an upwardly curved assembly of wedge-shaped units called *voussoirs* (Figure 6.9). The curve used by the Romans was a circle, which meant that all the wedge-shaped segments were identical, permitting easy fabrication. That is undoubtedly one reason they chose the circular form. Another is the simplicity of the *centering*, the wooden formwork on which the stone voussoirs are placed before the keystone locks them together so that the arch stands on its own.

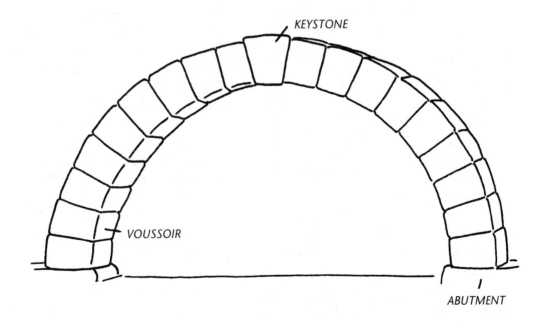

Figure 6.9

Build an Arch Bridge

MATERIALS

- 1 sheet of foam board, about 1 inch (25 mm) thick, 2 feet (600 mm) wide, and 2¹/₂ feet (750 mm) long (available at art supply stores)
- 1 sheet of foam board about 8 x 8 inches (200 x 200 mm)
- Ruler
- Pencil
- Craft knife
- Nail or pin
- Ball of string
- Cardboard
- Several heavy books

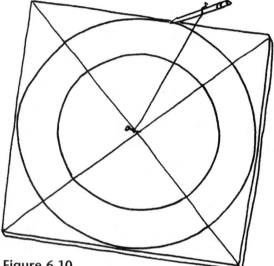

Figure 6.10

ADULT SUPERVISION RECOMMENDED.

🏛 On the long edge of the foam board mark off a line 6 inches (150 mm) from the end and cut off the segment with the knife. You will now have a square sheet of foam board. Using the ruler, draw two diagonal lines to locate the center of the square. Place a nail or pin in the center and attach one end of the string to it. Attach the other end of the string to the pencil so that the pencil will just touch the side of the board (Figure 6.10), and with the *compass* you have thus built, draw a large circle that just touches the four sides of the square. Now, measure off 2 inches (50 mm) from the outside circle and draw a smaller circle using the same procedure you used to draw the large circle. Cut the board in half so that you have two boards, each 1 x 2 feet (300 x 600 mm). Place a piece of cardboard under the foam so that you do not cut into the table or floor you are using as a cutting surface. Carefully cut each of the arches you have outlined on the boards. Divide each arch into seven sections. You can do this by eye, using a pencil to indicate the divisions. It does not have to be exact; after all, the stones used by the Romans were not all exactly the same size. Number the sections and cut them out. You now have the voussoirs for two arch bridges.

To construct an arch bridge, erect the two arches about 4 inches (100 mm) apart and place the 8 x 8-inch foam board on top of the two arches. Use wedges between the arches and the bottom of the board to hold the

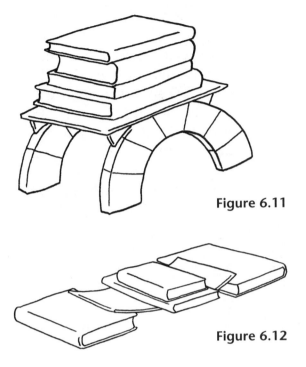

Figure 6.11

board in place (Figure 6.11). Carefully place a book on the platform and keep adding more books on top until the bridge collapses. Note how many books it takes to collapse the bridge.

To construct a beam bridge, place the 4 inch x 2 foot (100 mm x 600 mm) foam board between two books (Figure 6.12). This model is equivalent to the stone beam bridge built in Portugal. Next place a book in the center of this beam bridge and keep adding books until it breaks. Note how many books it takes.

Figure 6.12

Which bridge was stronger, the beam bridge or the arch bridge?

From the arch experiment, it is apparent that arches and beams support their loads in different ways. A beam supports loads primarily by bending. An arch in which the segments or voussoirs are not glued together still supports a load. However, the load-carrying capability of an arch clearly doesn't come from bending strength, since the separated segments have none. The arch therefore carries loads using only its compressive strength (Figure 6.13). Stone, which has good compressive strength but little tensile strength, is an ideal material for use in arch bridges.

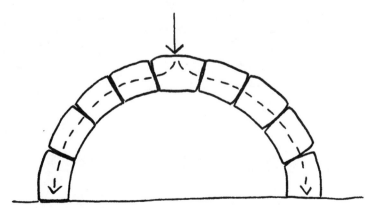

Figure 6.13

Some of the most famous ancient stone arch bridges are the Ponte Sant' Angelo on the Tiber River in Rome built in A.D. 134 by the emperor Hadrian, the Anji Bridge crossing the Xiao River built in China in the 6th century, and the Pont d'Avignon over the Rhone River built in the 12th century (Figure 6.14). Except for the Ponte Sant' Angelo, you will notice that none of the later bridges are semicircular in shape but rather form an arc that is a smaller part of a circle. In a semicircular arch, the base or *springing* is vertical since the curve begins with a vertical line. But if the circle is cut horizontally above the center, the springing lies at a shallow angle to the horizontal.

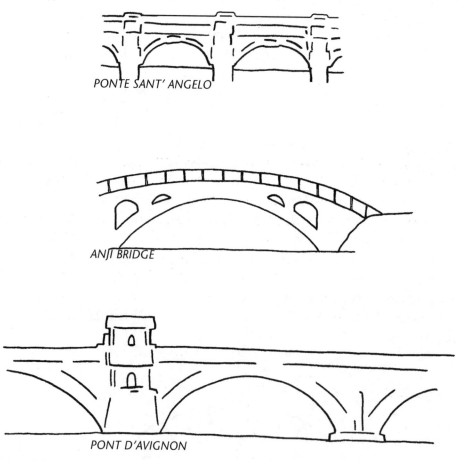

PONTE SANT' ANGELO

ANJI BRIDGE

PONT D'AVIGNON

Figure 6.14

Build a Shallow Arch

MATERIALS
- **5 foam voussoirs (see "Build an Arch Bridge" project in this chapter)**
- **2 heavy books**

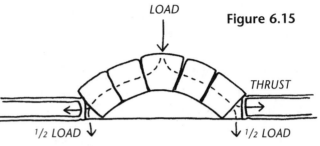

Figure 6.15

🏛 You can build a shallow arch using only five of the voussoirs you cut for the semicircular arch. Note that you need to hold the base of the arch to make it stand. You can do this by placing a book next to both bases against which the arch can push. This push is the *thrust* of the shallow arch (Figure 6.15). The books you need to hold the arch shape are equivalent to the massive masonry blocks that were employed in building real bridges such as the Pont d'Avignon.

The Pont du Gard in southern France is the best preserved of the Roman aqueducts (Figure 1.5). It was built in 18 B.C. by Marcus Agrippa and has three tiers of semicircular stone arches with the top ones carrying a water channel (Figure 6.16). It is a supreme example of the art of Roman bridge building.

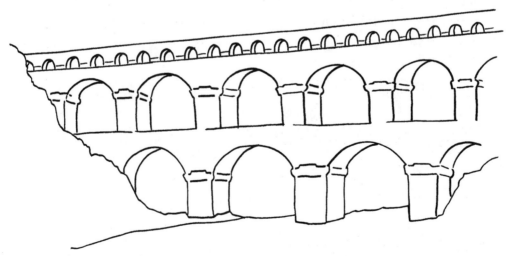

Figure 6.16

The span of early beam bridges was limited by the availability of natural materials. Arch bridges could achieve greater spans but were still limited by the need for massive masonry to keep the arch from splaying out. Also, laying the stone voussoirs on a wood form during construction was complicated and meant that a wooden bridge first had to be built to serve as the support for the stone bridge. Today, with the use of steel and reinforced concrete, many of these limitations no longer exist. Nevertheless, for longer spans, other types of bridges were needed.

Truss Bridges

The intrepid Romans undoubtedly thought of using short lengths of timber joined together in a series of triangles to create a truss. We can't see examples of these Roman truss bridges because the wood used in their construction rotted away long ago. The first records we have of truss bridges are in the writings of Andrea Palladio, a 16th-century Italian architect. Palladio describes a number of bridges he designed including a 100-foot-long (30 m) truss over the Cismone River that descends from the mountains that divide Italy and Germany.

Build a Triangular Truss

MATERIALS
- **Drill**
- **2 tongue depressors (available from a pharmacy)**
- **Brass paper fastener**
- **Rubber band**

ADULT SUPERVISION RECOMMENDED.

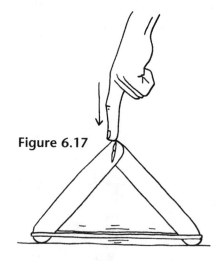

Figure 6.17

Have an adult drill small holes near the end of the tongue depressors. Connect two tongue depressors with the fastener and connect the other ends of the tongue depressors with a rubber band. The rubber band should be loose enough so that the two tongue depressors and the rubber band form a triangle, but not so loose that the rubber band falls off. Stand the assembly upright with the rubber band at the bottom. If you push the peak of the triangular assembly down you will notice that the rubber band stretches. This implies that the rubber band is in tension. The two legs of the triangle made of the rigid tongue depressors are in compression. This assembly of such tension and compression elements is called a *truss* (Figure 6.17).

In its simplest form, the truss is a set of three bars arranged in a triangular configuration. When used to support the roof of a house, the inclined bars are called the rafters and the horizontal bar is the tie beam. For a bridge, many such triangular units, trusses, need to be joined together. The Cismone Bridge, for instance, consists of 10 triangles arranged in six panels between vertical bars that Palladio called *colonelli* or "little columns" in Italian. (Figure 6.18).

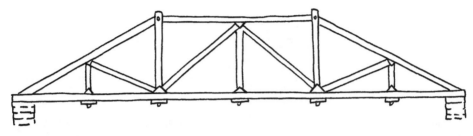

Figure 6.18

Build a Bridge Truss

MATERIALS
- **Drill**
- **10 tongue depressors**
- **Triangular truss (see "Build a Triangular Truss" project in this chapter)**
- **9 brass fasteners**

ADULT SUPERVISION RECOMMENDED.

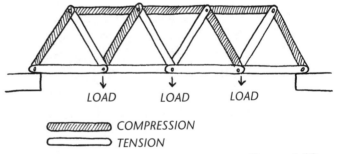

Figure 6.19

🏛 Have an adult drill small holes near the end of the tongue depressors. Remove the rubber band from your triangular truss and replace it with another tongue depressor. Continue to add another triangle with two more tongue depressors and another fastener. Keep adding more units until you achieve a four-bay bridge (Figure 6.19). The top bar of your truss, just like the top of a beam, is in compression and the bottom bar of the truss is in tension just like the bottom of the beam. The diagonal bars of the truss sloping toward the supports are in compression and the ones sloping away from the supports are in tension. Can you explain why?

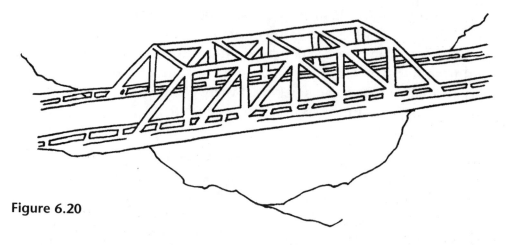

Figure 6.20

Trusses come in many shapes depending on their application. Some are located below the roadway and some above. Some are simple spans, meaning that they go from one support to another (Figure 6.20). Others are continuous, meaning that they span over three or more supports.

Cable Bridges

Long ago, people relied on the tensile strength of ropes made of vegetable fibers such as hemp to create bridges. By stretching a rope across a canyon or gorge and tying the ends firmly to a tree or boulder, they created a simple bridge. Of course they quickly found that they needed two more ropes to hold on to for stability before they could actually walk across their bridge (Figure 6.21). This idea was

Figure 6.21

used to build the first modern suspension bridge in 1826, the Menai Strait Bridge on the west coast of Wales. Instead of a rope, the designers assembled a chain with iron links 10 feet (3 m) long. To carry the bridge over the 570-foot (174 m-) strait, 80 such links were assembled together into a suspension chain. Soon after it was built, the bridge began to *oscillate* (vibrate like a violin string) when the wind was blowing. To cure the problem, the bridge was stiffened by making the deck heavier. The bridge served for the next 115 years before being replaced.

Curiously, the Britannia Bridge built across the Menai Stait 25 years after the chain bridge looks more like a beam bridge. In fact, this railroad bridge is a huge wrought iron box inside which the train travels. It was designed and built by Robert Stephenson, the man who designed the locomotive for his father's railroad (see chapter 5). A box is a perfectly logical shape for a beam, just like an *I* shape except that the extra material in a box beam is carved out of the inside instead of the sides (Figure 6.22).

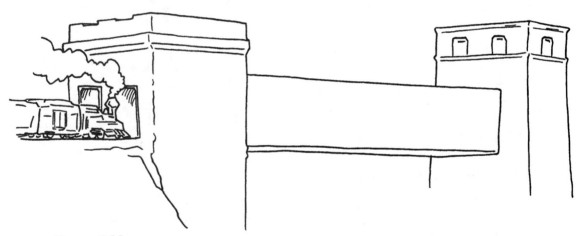

Figure 6.22

Build a Suspension Bridge

A suspension bridge consists of a pair of towers from which two cables or chains are hung; a number of cable or chain hangers; a deck; and anchors at either end to fasten the main cables or chains (Figure 6.23). These bridges are used to span the widest rivers and gorges.

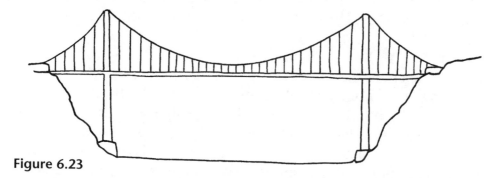

Figure 6.23

MATERIALS
- 3 sheets of cardboard, 8 x 14 inches (200 mm x 380 mm)
- Pencil
- Ruler
- Scissors
- Tape
- Stapler
- 4 brass fasteners
- Paper clips, enough to make a chain 5 feet long

Figure 6.24

To make a tower, mark the narrow side of one of the sheets of cardboard at 1 inch, 4 inches, and 5 inches (25, 100, and 125 mm). Draw lines at these points parallel to the long sides and fold the cardboard along these lines. On the two wide faces, draw a 2-inch x 4-inch (50- x 100-mm) opening about 5 inches (125 mm) from one end. This will be where the deck of the bridge will pass through (Figure 6.24). Cut these holes with the scissors. Tape the long edges together to finish your tower. Make an identical second tower. To make the bridge deck, fold one of the cardboards in half longitudinally (along its edge) and fold it once more. Cut along the fold lines. You should have four strips of cardboard that are 2 inches (50 mm) wide. Lay these end to end with a small overlap that allows you to staple them together. You should have a bridge deck that's about 50 inches long,

Figure 6.25

or about 4¹/₂ feet long. To make the chain, string together paper clips to a length of about 5 feet (1.5 m) (Figure 6.25).

Assemble the bridge by placing the two towers at least 2¹/₂ feet (750 mm) apart on a table, attaching the chains with fasteners to the tower, and clamping the backstays (the part of the chain between the tower and the anchor) of the chain between books (Figure 6.26). Slide the deck through the holes in the towers. Hang the deck girders from the chains by starting at the center of the bridge and working alternately toward each of the towers. Adjust the length of the hangers to keep the deck horizontal. You can experiment by loading the bridge and noting at what point the anchors slip because there aren't enough books (which act as anchors) piled onto the chain.

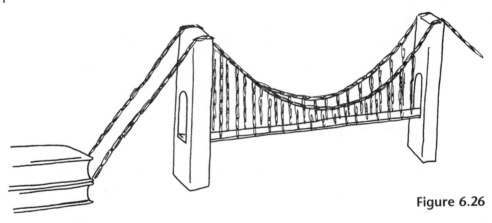

Figure 6.26

Modern suspension bridges are built with cables assembled by wrapping together many thin wires (each with a diameter of about ¹/₄ inch (5 mm). These cables are similar to those first used by John Roebling in the mid-19th century. Roebling was the man who designed and built New York City's Brooklyn Bridge in 1887; the bridge set a record with its 1,595-foot (464 m) span. Looking into the future, Roebling predicted that suspension bridges with spans exceeding 3,000 feet (1000 m) would be built within 100 years. Engineers proved him right, but it happened within 50 years with the construction of the 3,500-foot (1050-m) George Washington Bridge in 1937. Today, the longest suspension bridge is the 6,530-foot (1991-m) Akashi-Kaikyo Bridge connecting the main island of Honshu to Shikoku in Japan. This bridge is so long that it is affected by the earth's curvature. Each of its 925-foot (282-m) towers is perpendicular to the ground; but, since the earth is curved, the towers are not parallel to each other (Figure 6.27).

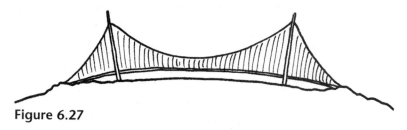

Figure 6.27

Cable-Stayed Bridges

It took almost 200 years for an old idea to bear fruit. In 1784 German carpenter C. J. Löscher proposed using a timber stay, a wooden arm used for support, to hang a timber bridge from a timber tower. Later, instead of using timber for the stay someone suggested using chains. Later still, someone else proposed cables (Figure 6.28). Unfortunately,

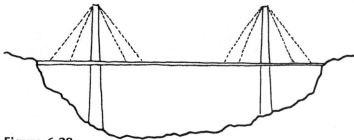

Figure 6.28

some of these early cable-stayed bridges collapsed, one as a result of a chain link breaking when the bridge started swaying in the wind. Although a number of early suspension bridges also failed due to twisting because of blowing wind (Figure 6.29), a famous French engineer, Claude Navier, condemned cable-stayed bridges but not suspension bridges. Since Navier was such an important and highly respected engineer, his pronouncement resulted in only suspension bridges being built for the next 100 years, until after World War II in the late 1940s. During WWII, most of the bridges crossing the Rhine River in Germany were destroyed and had to rebuilt quickly. German engineer F. Dischinger had rediscovered cable-stayed bridges in 1938 and used the idea to design a railroad bridge over the Elbe River in Germany.

Compared to a suspension bridge, a cable-stayed bridge transfers loads directly to the supporting tower rather than indirectly, first through a suspender cable and then to the main cable (Figure 6.30). Such bridges are particularly suited to span 500 to 1,200 feet (150 to

Figure 6.29

360 m) while suspension bridges are better suited for longer spans. This middle range was exactly what was needed to span across the Rhine River after the war and Dischinger was asked to participate in the design of many of these. A total of 13 such bridges were soon built in Germany.

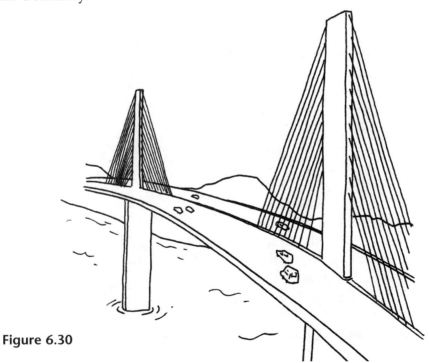

Figure 6.30

Build a Cable-Stayed Bridge

MATERIALS
- **3 sheets of stiff cardboard, each 10 x 12 inches (250 x 300 mm)**
- **Pencil**
- **Stapler**
- **Scissors**
- **Hole puncher**
- **Carpet thread**
- **Glue**

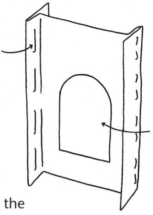

Figure 6.31

To make an *I*-shaped tower, mark the narrow side of one of the sheets of cardboard at 2, 3, 7, and 8 inches. Draw lines at these points parallel to the long sides and fold the cardboard along these lines. Staple the cardboard where it overlaps one inch. Do this for both sides. Draw a 2 x 3-inch opening about 3 inches from one end. This will be where the deck of the bridge will pass through. Cut the hole with the scissors. Make an identical second tower.

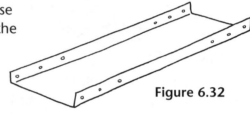

Figure 6.32

Cut the remaining sheet in half to obtain two narrow sheets. Fold up the edges of these two sheets to form beams along the edges (Figure 6.32). Punch three small holes into the edge beams about 1½ inches (35 mm) apart from each end. Passing under the deck as shown, place a length of thread, about 16 inches (800 mm) long, through each of these holes (Figure 6.33). Pass a deck section through the hole in each of the towers. Extend the threads on each side of the bridge to the top of the towers and tie the threads (Figure 6.34). Adjust the length of thread so that the deck is level. When you have assembled both

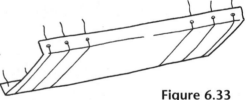

Figure 6.33

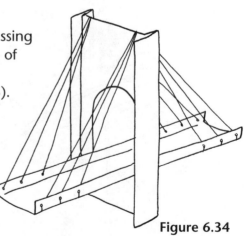

Figure 6.34

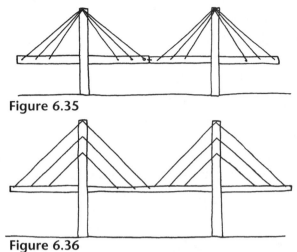

Figure 6.35

Figure 6.36

towers and decks, staple the end of one deck to the other to finish your cable-stayed bridge (Figure 6.35).

Notice that when you push down the center of the span, the cables tighten and try to lift up the side spans. If the bridge deck is made of one continuous material, both the center and side spans are in fact balanced on the tower. When a car begins to cross the bridge, that balance is upset and it is up to the bridge designer to add stiffness by making the deck strong enough.

The bridge you have built has an arrangement of cables in the form of a fan. It is also possible to arrange the cables in the form of a harp, with all the cables parallel to each other (Figure 6.36). Many beautiful bridges have been built using the cable-stayed principle. Two particularly dramatic bridges are the Sunshine Skyway in Florida, which spans 1,200 feet (350 m), and the Normandy Bridge in France, which spans 2,800 feet (856 m).

Moveable Bridges

In addition to all these fixed bridges there are also moveable bridges. These take the form of vertical lift bridges, bascule bridges, or swing or tilt bridges. The reason for introducing a complicated mechanism needed for a moveable bridge is to open a waterway to let ships pass.

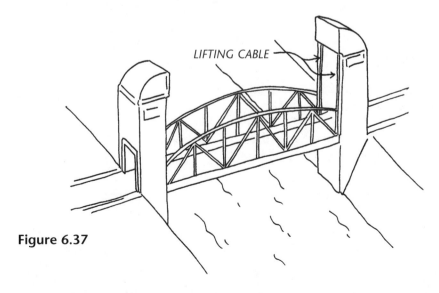

LIFTING CABLE

Figure 6.37

A vertical lift bridge, such as New York City's Roosevelt Island bridge, has two towers from which a deck hangs that can be raised or lowered with cables (Figure 6.37). In a swing bridge, the deck pivots or swings aside to allow ships to pass on either side (Figure 6.38). In a bascule bridge, the deck, balanced by a counterweight, tilts upward (Figure 6.39). A double bascule such as the 1,600 foot (500 m) London Tower Bridge has two tilting decks. The London Tower Bridge's decks open simultaneously in less than two minutes.

Now that we have presented the story of bridges, you can appreciate why there are so many different types, each with its own shape and purpose to span a river, a canyon, or even part of the ocean.

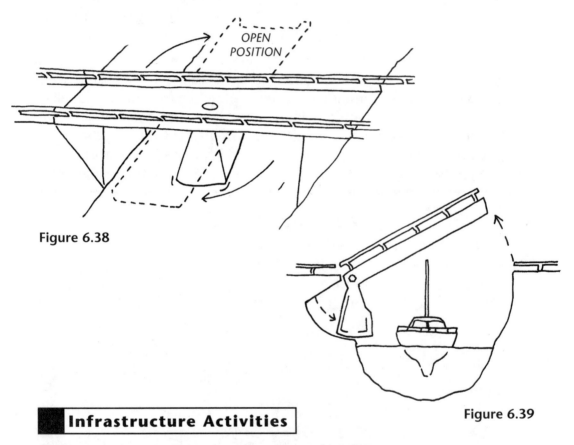

OPEN POSITION

Figure 6.38

Figure 6.39

Infrastructure Activities

🏛 Draw a time line that shows how the span of bridges has increased over the years since the time of the log bridge.

7

Wires, Wires Everywhere

According to legend, a young shepherd on Crete, an island in the Aegean Sea, was walking in a field about 600 B.C. when suddenly he had difficulty lifting his foot off the ground. His iron-tacked sandals seemed to be stuck to the ground. To find what was causing this, he dug down and found a stone that was strongly attracted to his sandals. He had discovered a *lodestone*, which possesses the mysterious attractive property of *magnetism*.

The young Cretan then picked up two lodestones and found that they stuck to each other. Being of an inquisitive nature, the boy pulled the stones apart and turned one over. Now he was unable to bring the two stones together because they repelled each other. Incredibly, magnetism involves both attraction and repulsion. Equally baffling was another discovery of the ancient Greeks. Rubbing a piece of amber, a fossil resin, with a soft cloth created an electrical attraction that could make hair stand on end when the amber was brought close (the word *electricity*, incidentally, comes from *electron*, the Greek word for amber). These two curious and mysterious phenomena were not explained for thousands of years, yet they are the basis for all the electric conveniences we take for granted today. Many scientists and inventors worked to make electricity a practical and useful tool for modern living. One such person was Benjamin Franklin, who, among other things, showed that lightning was an electrical phenomenon.

Visualizing Magnetism

MATERIALS
- Iron filings (obtain these from a hobby store)
- 1 sheet of cardboard or stiff paper
- 1 magnet, any size

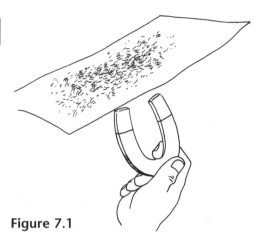

Figure 7.1

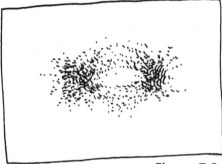

Figure 7.2

Sprinkle a small quantity of iron filings on the paper and place the magnet under the paper (Figure 7.1). Gently tap the paper and note how the iron filings arrange themselves (Figure 7.2). The pattern of curved lines on the paper is a visual representation of the lines of the electromagnetic force.

Before electricity could be used, electric power had to be produced. Michael Faraday, a British scientist, demonstrated how to do this in 1831. Faraday built a device that consisted of a copper disc mounted

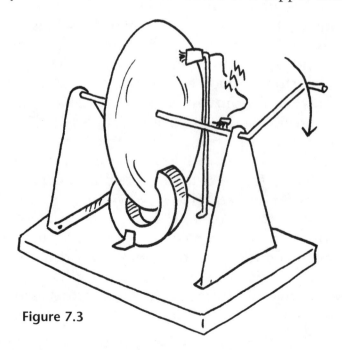

Figure 7.3

on a shaft that was placed vertically between the poles of a magnet. He then connected one end of a wire to a metal brush in contact with the outside edge of the disc and the other end to a metal brush rubbing against the center shaft. By rotating the disc with a crank, he generated an electrical current in the wire (Figure 7.3). Essentially, he was converting the mechanical energy of the rotating disc into electrical energy in the wire. Huge generators are built today to supply the power needed for lighting, running motors, and providing heat and air conditioning. These generators are powered by steam engines fueled by coal or oil or run with water turbines. Some are even fueled with renewable sources of energy such as the wind, sun, *biomass* (chopped-up wood or plant matter), or geothermal energy (See chapter 10).

Faraday also demonstrated the principle of an electric motor, which is essentially the opposite of a generator since it converts electricity into mechanical energy. It had been demonstrated a century earlier that electricity could be transmitted through a wire. Combined with the generator and the motor, electricity suddenly became practical.

The First Wires

The first invention that resulted in wires being strung through the countryside was the telegraph. Samuel Morse, a genius who was also a talented painter, together with Alfred Vail developed a method of sending messages through wires by opening and closing the circuit, that is, by letting the electricity either flow or stop flowing through the wire. In order to make his machine work, Morse developed a code, substituting dots and pauses for the letters of the alphabet and numbers. These dots and pauses were later changed to dots and dashes-what we now call the Morse code (Figure 7.4). Morse also needed a

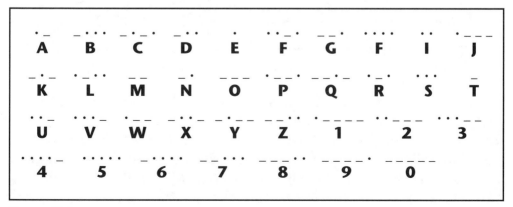

Figure 7.4

sending device, which was simply a key used to open or close the circuit to create the dots, and a recording device that would mark the dots on a paper tape (Figure 7.5).

The first telegraph line was strung in 1838 between Washington, D.C., and Baltimore, Maryland, a distance of 40 miles (64 km). Within a short time, lines were sprouting all over the world, connecting distant cities and speeding the transmission of news and messages. Within 20 years, cables were even laid under the oceans, connecting the continents of the world for the first time. This was an incredible revolution in the speed of communication, because before the telegraph, messages were sent with the speed of a horse (or a ship) and thereafter were received as fast as the telegraph operator could tap the key. In 1863, one such telegraph operator was the young Thomas Edison, who would soon revolutionize how we see.

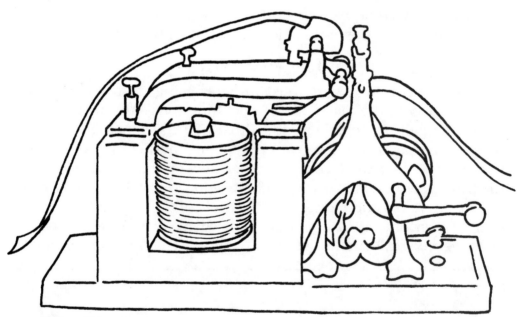

Figure 7.5

In the year before telegraph wires crossed the wild, western United States, *Pony Express* riders picked up messages in Missouri and rode west to California in relay fashion. Each rider would go about 90 miles (150 km), changing horses about every 20 miles (30 km) before passing his *mochila* to the next rider. The *mochila*, a Spanish word for "knapsack," was a pair of leather pouches that hung on either side of the horse's saddle and contained about 30 pounds (15 kg) of messages. By taking shortcuts and avoiding poorly built roads, the Pony Express easily beat the slower overland stagecoach. In this way, the 1,900-mile (3,000-km) journey was completed in about eight days, a tremendous improvement over the month-long journey by stagecoach. In 1861, after only 18 months in operation, 80 riders were out of a job as the Pony Express was discontinued, having been supplanted by the completion of the telegraph over the same route. Telegraph messages were then delivered in seconds!

Wire Connections

How many wires does it take to connect nine houses?

MATERIALS
• **1 sheet of paper**
• **Pencil or pen**

🏛 On a blank sheet of paper, draw nine dots, three rows of three dots spaced widely apart. Number the dots and start by connecting dot 1 to each of the other dots with a straight or curved line (Figure 7.6). Repeat the process with dot 2, noting that you don't have to connect dot 2 to dot 1 since they are already connected. Count all the connections you have drawn. You should end up with 36 separate wires. That's an awful lot of wires to connect just nine houses. A clever individual suggested another way: Why not channel all communications through a central distribution point so that instead of 36 wires you needed only 9 wire connections (Figure 7.7).

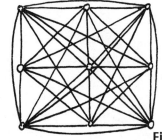

Figure 7.6

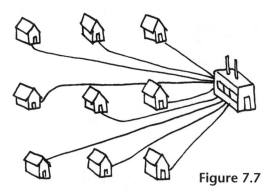

Figure 7.7

By combining the telegraph with a typewriting machine, written messages that were encoded by the sending machine were decoded by the receiving machine. The result was a written strip of paper, the *telegram,* on which was written the original message in its original language. Now there were two reasons for stringing wire—the telegraph and the telegram. But if only one could speak and be heard through the wires!

More Wires

Because his mother was deaf, Alexander Graham Bell started his career by teaching deaf children to speak. He was desperate to understand how sound is transmitted from one medium, such as air, to another, such as the eardrum. He knew that sound traveled through the air as vibrations from the mouth of the speaker to the ear of the listener and that these vibrations caused the air to compress and expand (changing its density). "If I could make a current of electricity vary precisely as the air varies in density during the production of sound," he wrote, "I should be able to transmit speech telegraphically." In 1876, when Bell was 29 years old, he developed what he called his "electrical speech machine." He started experimenting and building and testing such a machine, and one day, since he was an incredibly clumsy man, he spilled some battery acid. He cried out into the machine, calling his assistant, Thomas Watson, in another room, "Watson, come here! I need you." Watson heard this, though not too clearly, and for the first time, words had been transmitted through a wire, giving birth to the *telephone*!

More wires were strung between houses and central exchanges in the city and then across the country, connecting its cities, and even across the ocean floor, connecting continents.

Make a Simple Telephone

MATERIALS
- **Pin**
- **2 small paper cups**
- **13-foot (4-m) length of carpet thread**

Using the pin, make a hole in the bottom of each cup. Thread one end of the thread through the bottom of the cup and make a double or triple

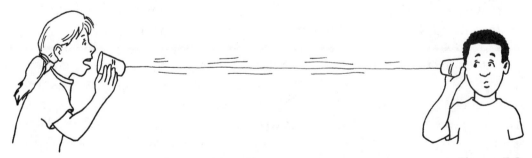

Figure 7.8

knot on the inside of the cup so that the thread will not slip through the hole. Do this for the other cup using the other end of the thread. Ask your friend to hold one cup and stand at one end of a room or outdoors and hold the other cup so that the string is taut (but don't pull so hard that the thread pulls out of the cup). Hold your cup by the rim to your ear and ask your friend to speak softly into the other cup while holding it by the rim (Figure 7.8). You should be able to hear what your friend says.

As you spoke into the cup, the bottom vibrated in measure with the tones of your speech. The string then transmitted these vibrations to the other cup, whose bottom was set into vibration. Finally, the vibrations of the bottom of the cup were sent out through the air to your friend's ear.

Light

After the sun set in the nighttime sky, the only way our early ancestors could see, at least at first, was to use the light of a wood fire and later by lighting the wick of a candle made of wax obtained from a honeycomb. Even in ancient times, though, lamps using oil became the custom and were used for 2,000 years. Oil lamps with wicks of cotton lit the interior of all buildings until the early 18th century when the use of coal gas gave rise to the need for a distribution system using pipes buried in the city streets. Every day at sundown, crews of lamp lighters would fan out along city streets to light the gas lanterns. Gas lamps were employed throughout the 18th century and into the early 20th century even after an invention that was to give us light with a flick of a switch.

Thomas Edison had grown tired of moving from place to place, working as a "tramp telegrapher," and so he settled in Boston. There he studied Faraday's writings on electricity. At the age of 21, he filed his first patent for a vote recorder. It was not very practical, and he was unable to sell it, so he decided to only work on inventions that he was sure could be sold. Within two years, he had designed a stock ticker that brokers could have in their offices to read the latest stock prices. It was a big hit. With the money he received, he set up a laboratory in Menlo Park, New Jersey, to begin a very organized search for new ideas. He engaged a team of assistants to help him, including machinists, designers, and technicians. Together they developed dozens of inventions.

The invention of which Edison was the proudest was the *phonograph*. The first phonograph used a needle riding on a cylinder covered

THE EVOLUTION OF RECORDING

Phonograph discs were improved over the years until the introduction of the 33 revolutions per minute (rpm) disc in the 1950s. That was soon replaced by magnetic tapes on which the sound was recorded by magnetizing the iron coating on the tape. Today, tapes have, for the most part, been replaced by compact discs, which use laser light to read coded microscopic pits that have been burned into the disc by another laser.

with tinfoil. When speaking into the instrument, the needle vibrated and the vibrations were scratched into the foil (Figure 7.9). The needle transmitted the vibrations that had been scratched into the cylinder to a horn. The sound quality was poor, but it worked!

Edison kept developing inventions having to do with sound. In the process, he developed a carbon button transmitter that is still used today in telephone handsets. The idea was very simple. Granules of carbon were placed in a button-sized container into which two wires were placed. The wires were then connected to an electric line. When speaking into the button, the carbon particles were either compressed or spread apart, allowing more or less current to flow through the wire. It was similar to Bell's telephone transmitter but worked much better.

Figure 7.9

While studying what could be done with electricity, Edison decided to tackle the problem of developing an electric light. He worked on the whole system, from generator to wire distribution to house wiring to the light bulb itself. He first decided that he would wire a house so that each light was independent of the next, which is known as *parallel circuitry* (Figure 7.10). This meant that the failure of one light would not cause all the lights to turn off. There had been some light experiments before Edison, but they had not resulted in a

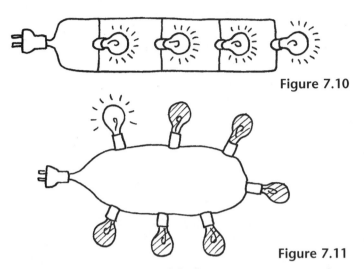

Figure 7.10

Figure 7.11

practical system because most used lights in a series so that one bad bulb darkened the whole string (Figure 7.11). To find a practical light bulb was not easy and involved finding the right filament, the element that glows inside the bulb. It also required creating a vacuum inside the glass, placing the delicate filament inside the bulb, and then sealing the bulb so that air would not enter. After a thousand attempts, Edison came close to success, by using a carbonized thread in the shape of a horseshoe, but that light burned for only two hours (to make the carbonized thread, it was baked in an oven until it turned black, just like burned toast). Finally, a filament of carbonized bamboo was tested and it burned for more than a month. Edison was called the "Wizard of Menlo Park" for inventing the electric light.

At first, only neighborhoods had lights. Then whole cities had lights, and eventually lights stretched across the countryside. This meant more and more wires. Soon the cities were choked with wires strung between buildings and between poles that sprouted from the sidewalks. All these wires were delicate; consequently, in a big wind or an ice storm, they would break and drop to the ground. After a blizzard that struck New York City in 1888, the city moved the wires underground. Then the city's residents could once more look up at the sky without having a spiderweb of wires in the way.

Except for wires that still stretch across the countryside to provide electric power and telephone connections, almost all cables in cities are now carried in underground conduits and undersea cables connect continents. There are still some overhead wires in the less-populated areas of cities. When you flip a switch to start your computer or turn on a light or your television set, the power that flows through the wires in your home may have traveled thousands of miles. It may have been generated in a power plant or a hydro-electric plant or come from wind turbines, photoelectric cells that convert sunlight directly into electricity, or even from burned garbage. After power is generated, the electricity is transformed to increase its *voltage*, its potential energy, which is boosted to about 200kV, or 200,000 volts, through transmission lines.

Electric power is measured in volts and amperes. If you think of the flow of electricity like water in a river, voltage is the potential energy as measured by the difference in height between two points along the length of the river. Amperage is the current or speed of the water. The power is the total amount of water flowing past a point in the river that is equivalent to the product of volts multiplied by amperes. Therefore, for the same amount of power, if you increase the voltage, you decrease the amperes. In a very flat river, equivalent to low voltage, water has to flow very quickly to create a large amount of power. Wires carrying a high amperage will waste electrical power by turning it into heat, which is similar to fast-flowing water wasting a lot of its power by rubbing against the riverbed and riversides. Therefore, transmission lines need to carry a high voltage (a steep river) and are called high-tension lines.

When the power reaches your town or city, the voltage is then transformed downward to between 12 and 35kV. Finally, just before it enters your house, it is again transformed further down to the 120-240 volts in your house wires.

All these utility lines for electricity, telephone, and television cables as well as water, gas, and sewer lines are generally separated and follow their own path along a street. This is why you may see the electric company dig up the street one week, the water company digging it up the next week, and maybe the telephone company the following week. City dwellers have been generally unhappy with this uncoordinated arrangement of utilities. Walt Disney had a better idea—why not put all utilities in a single large underground tunnel so that, as wires have to be changed or pipes replaced, the workers can make the changes within the tunnel without having to constantly rip up the street? Disney built Disney World in Florida with the all utilities in a single tunnel to demonstrate the benefits of such a system (Figure 7.12).

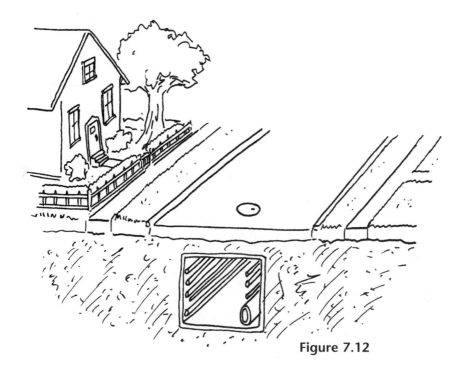

Figure 7.12

Wireless

The next great invention was Guglielmo Marconi's wireless telegraph. Instead of transmitting electric signals through wires, Marconi generated electromagnetic waves that traveled through the air. In 1901, he succeeded in sending a signal using Morse code across the Atlantic Ocean from a sending station in Cornwall, England, to Newfoundland, Canada. Only 12 years later, Edwin Armstrong developed the first practical voice transmitter and the *radio* was born. Soon thereafter, there was *television*, and a picture as well as a voice could be transmitted through the air. Now there are wireless telephones, beepers, and Internet message units.

Today, we have to look far out in space to find the farthest part of our infrastructure. In space are satellites that relay signals between two points on Earth for television and telephones and the Internet. Satellites eliminate the need for direct wire connections. Together with computers and the labor-saving devices in our homes, these fantastic developments have improved our lives but have resulted in more electrical power being needed. Therefore, more and heavier wires are now required to transmit this power. Since the late 19th century, new fiber-optic cables, using light waves passing through a glass fiber cable, are used to transmit sounds and images. Alexander

Graham Bell realized in 1860 that sounds could be transmitted by reflecting light on a mirror that vibrated with the sound of his voice. The light was then focused with lenses onto a selenium plate that measured the changes in light intensity caused by the vibrating mirror. This plate was wired to a speaker to allow the voice to be heard. The device was crude, and because the light was sent through the air, it only worked over a short distance. When the medium for transmission was changed in the mid-19th century from air to a very pure, thin, glass (silica) fiber and the light source was concentrated as a *laser*, it became possible to transmit sound around the world through fiber-optic cables. The world of our infrastructure is constantly changing.

As you sit in front of your computer, consider what each of your keystrokes does. First, electricity is providing the power you need to operate the computer. As you press down on a key, you are closing a circuit, allowing electricity to flow that identifies a particular letter or number. When you type in an Internet address, you are connecting to a server, another computer somewhere in the world that channels your request. You may instantly reach thousands of other computers, one of which may have the information you seek filed on its electronic disc, which then becomes instantly available to you. Time and distance have been compressed by the invention of the Internet.

Infrastructure Activities

In a transformer, an insulated wire is wound around an iron core. A second wire with fewer revolutions is then wound around the same core. The transformer works by electromagnetic *induction*, with the voltage in the two wires proportional to the number of windings. How many windings are needed on each side of the transformer to reduce a high-tension voltage to your house voltage?

Use a prism, a triangular piece of glass, to break down light from the sun into its spectrum, a rainbow of colors. Note that the colors go from deep red to orange, yellow, green, blue, purple, to violet. At either end of the spectrum there are colors you cannot see, infrared and ultraviolet. Infrared light is used to operate the remote control of your television. Where else is it used?

Computers use a digital language that corresponds to a switch being on or off (or, 0 and 1). Notice how that is similar to the Morse code with its dots (0) and dashes (1). Make up a code using 0 and 1 to identify all the letters of the alphabet or create your own code that can be used by a computer.

8
What Happens When I Flush the Toilet?

You have just let the water flow out of the sink or flushed the toilet. Imagine the path this water will now take. If you look under the sink, you will notice that the pipe carrying the water doesn't go straight down but makes a detour, going back up before continuing downward. This detour is a water trap and is meant to keep dangerous gases from flowing up the pipe into your home. After this little detour, the pipe turns into the wall or drops through the floor and disappears from view, continuing down and ending in the basement of your house or apartment building. There, it connects to a larger pipe that slopes down toward the basement wall and again disappears through the wall. This pipe continues under the sidewalk or front yard and under the street where it connects to a sewer (Figure 8.1). A sewer is an underground pipe, larger than all the pipes that attach to it, that carries the waste to a plant where solids are removed. There, the remaining dirty water is treated and purified to remove dangerous chemicals before being sent down into the ground, out to a river, or to the sea. This path from sink to sea was not always so neat and simple.

Civilizations as long as 5,000 years ago such as the Indus Valley peoples of Asia had complex sewer systems. However, all that was forgotten by the Middle Ages. Before the 19th century, most of the cities of the world stank because of inadequate sewer systems. The French

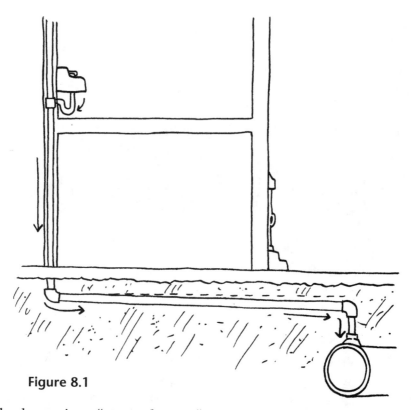

Figure 8.1

in Paris had a saying, "tout a la rue," meaning that all waste—including urine and feces-were thrown into the street. The sewer, which means "seaward" in old English, was merely a ditch in the center of the street that flowed toward the river. In some European towns, the second floor projected out beyond the ground floor. This was so that when chamber pots (there were no toilets) were emptied out the window and into the street, passersby could walk under the overhang and be protected from being drenched.

Indoor plumbing and toilets did not exist until the invention of the flush toilet in 1775. Only royalty and rich people could afford such an extravagance. The rest of the population still used ceramic chamber pots, which were sometimes placed under a padded seat. In the country, there was the privy, an enclosed wooden shack in which there was a wooden board with a hole placed over a pit in the earth. Flush toilets installed in a separate water closet became common only in the early 20th century. In older houses, spare bedrooms were then converted to bathrooms with sinks and toilets.

The problem with this dirty system of waste thrown into the street was that liquid sewage that flowed in the unpaved streets mixed with the soil to create a smelly, muddy mess. In fact, in 13th-century Paris, the smell was so bad that King Philip Augustus ordered the roads to be paved to cut down on the mud. This improved the situation, but then the sewage flowed down the streets toward the Seine River. As the population of the city increased, there came a time when the river became so clogged with garbage, sewage, and even dead bodies that Francois I, in 1539, ordered all home owners to build *cesspools* under their houses (Figure 8.2). Cesspools are underground tanks that are usually buried under a lawn but in cities were built in basements right under houses. Human waste that accumulated in these cesspools was collected and carted out of the city to dumps where the liquids seeped into the ground and the solids were allowed to ferment into "poudrette," a fertilizer that was valued as nourishment for soil on farms. To cut down on the bad odors, the dumps were moved very far from the city.

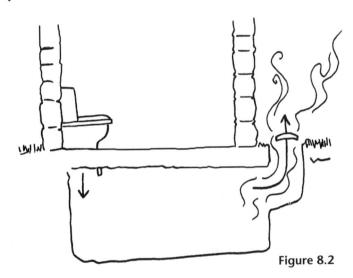

Figure 8.2

But the gases that built up in cesspools under houses continued to create problems. The worst smells came mostly from hydrogen sulfide, a gas that smells like rotten eggs. But one of the most deadly gases was carbon monoxide, which has no odor. (Carbon monoxide is one of the gases that comes out of the tailpipe of a car, which is the reason it is important not to run a car in an enclosed space like a garage.) The occupants of houses would often become ill from these gases. Sometimes, if someone lit a match to light a candle, the house would blow up because of the presence of methane, another gas. The most serious problems, though, were periodic cholera epidemics.

Cholera is a disease caused by food or water being infected by bacteria that comes from human waste or feces. Two of the major symptoms of the disease are diarrhea and vomiting, which cause the body to dehydrate, or lose too much water. Back then, cholera was almost always fatal. The epidemic of 1832, for instance, killed 20,000 Parisians. Today, by replacing body fluids through intravenous feeding (dripping a liquid with sugar and salt directly into the body's bloodstream), cholera can usually be cured.

Something had to be done to stop this periodic cycle of disease and death. The world's major European cities such as Paris and London turned to an old idea that had been used by the Minoans, a civilization that existed 4,000 years ago and thrived on the island of Crete in the Mediterranean Sea. The Minoans gathered rainwater into cisterns, large water tanks located on the hills above the capital city of Knossos. From the cisterns, the water was led through aqueducts to bathrooms where it was used to flush away human waste into *sewers*, terra cotta pipes that were joined together with cement. Of course the Minoans didn't just press a lever to flush away waste, but water simply flowed all the time, ensuring a degree of cleanliness and an odor-free atmosphere.

How Fast Does Water Need to Flow to Move Solid Waste?

MATERIALS
- **Stream or river**
- **Short stick**
- **Watch with a second hand**

ADULT SUPERVISION RECOMMENDED.

The velocity of water is controlled by two factors—the amount of water flowing through a channel and the slope of the channel. If you live near a river or a stream, you can easily determine its speed. To do so, measure out a 30-foot (10-m) distance along the riverbank. You can do this by pacing out the distance, having first measured the length of one of your paces. Next, toss a short stick into the water at the beginning of your measured length while at the same time looking at the second hand of your watch. Run to the end of your measured distance and note the time it takes the stick to reach that point. For instance, if it took 20 seconds for the stick to travel the distance, divide the measured distance by 20 to obtain the water velocity: Velocity = 30 ft/20 sec = 1½ ft/sec. Tests have shown that a velocity of 2 ft/sec (²/₃ m/sec) is sufficient to move waste along in a sewer.

How Waste Moves

You can also perform a simple experiment in a kitchen sink to see how waste moves.

MATERIALS
- **1 center of a paper towel roll**
- **Spoonful of soil**

Holding the tube horizontally, place the soil inside one end of the tube. Keeping the tube in a horizontal position, hold the end with the soil under slowly running water and note that the soil-water mixture spreads out but does not flow out. Now, slowly tilt the tube so that the water runs faster inside the tube. Note at what tilt angle all the soil is cleaned out of the tube. As you increase the tilt of the tube, you increase the velocity of the water.

In the middle of the 19th century, Baron Georges Haussmann, a city planner, created major avenues in Paris radiating from major squares (these were actually circles). To accomplish this, he cut new streets and widened old streets throughout Paris, demolishing many old houses and neighborhoods but creating a city with a less-crowded appearance. At the same time, new sewers were built that were so fancy that during the 1867 exposition, tours were led by white-gloved sewer men pushing boats full of elegantly dressed visitors. Even today, if you visit Paris you can take a tour through its sewers.

The shape of sewers is important. We learned from the experiment in chapter 1 that water channels have a natural shape (Fig. 1.6). The same is true for a sewer, but here the best shape is one that results in the lowest water velocity needed to prevent solids from settling. To understand this, consider the problem of a given amount of water moving along a channel. When the channel is wide like a river, water moves slowly. If the same amount of water moves through a narrow gorge, it moves faster because the same amount of water has to squeeze through a tighter space. Long ago, the engineers who designed sewers observed this and shaped the first sewers as vertical ovals (Figure 8.3). They also found that, by squeezing the bottom of the oval into an egg shape (Figure 8.4), the water moved faster at the bottom even when a small amount of sewage was flowing.

To keep a sewer flushed out, water has to be moving constantly, so sewers have to slope and cannot be horizontal. Imagine what that

Figure 8.3   **Figure 8.4**

means in a large modern city. Many different branches of a sewer coming from many different directions have to be precisely calculated so that each branch has sufficient slope and yet, when all the branches meet, they come together at the same elevation. A sewer system is like the branches of a man-made tree on its side that come together into a trunk that is a really big sewer. The city of Boston, for instance, has about 5,000 miles (9,000 km) of local sewers that if stretched out could cross the United States twice.

Because the city of London is on the banks of the Thames River, it is affected by tides; that is, its water level rises at high tide and drops at low tide. Tides are the result of the gravitational pull of the moon on the oceans. When the moon is directly above an ocean, it acts like a magnet to raise the water level. The water near a river's mouth, where it spills into the ocean, can also be affected by tides. When the tide is high, water from the river cannot flow out. It backs up, causing the river's water level to rise.

The streets of London are actually 30 feet (10 meters) below the high tide level of the Thames River, which means that at very high tides, water from the city's sewers could not flow into the river and would back up into the streets. That is what happened in 1858, when "The Great Stink" caused thousands to flee the city to avoid both the smell and the danger of death from cholera. To avoid this problem in the future, Marc Brunel, a great engineer, proposed to dig a tunnel under the Thames to drain the city to a lower section of the river. When the 1,600-foot (480-m) long tunnel was built, Queen Victoria ordered a mini rail line to be built inside to carry the dedication party. The grand opening was such a success that the tunnel became a tourist attraction lined with souvenir shops and never did serve as the city's drain. Eventually, it became part of London's subway system. During this time, Joseph Bazalgette, another engineer, built 100 miles (160 km) of sewers in the city that led to a better-smelling environment and a halt to the further spread of cholera.

Not all sewers end up as tourist attractions. For instance, Boston's sewers flow into 230 miles (370 km) of trunk (also called interceptor) sewers that lead to a plant where the sewage is cleaned. Most of the city's sewage used to flow into Boston Harbor. With a new awareness of the damage that this caused to the environment, the city built tunnels leading to a new sewage treatment plant on an island in the harbor. In the treatment plant, the solids are separated and then microbes (microscopic germs) are used to do most of the work of cleaning the remaining wastewater. The *sludge,* or solids produced by sewage treatment, is placed in tanks called digesters that remove dangerous and smelly gases. This leaves a purified material that is then disposed of in landfills or on the ocean floor. At the end of the process, disinfectants are added to the liquid, making it almost pure enough to drink, before it is released into the ocean. Most cities and towns in the world now treat their sewage and clean it before releasing the *effluent,* the remaining water, into streams, rivers, or the earth.

9

Where Does All the Garbage Go?

At First

Twenty thousand years ago, our ancestors caught fish, hunted wild animals, and gathered herbs, nuts, roots, and berries for food. They used animal skins for clothing and shelter. They made tools for sewing, hunting, carving, and grinding. It seems rather unlikely that they would leave any garbage. However, if you believe this, you would be wrong.

Only because our ancestors disposed of things that they couldn't eat or use do we know anything about them. *Archaeologists*, the scientists who dig in the ground, look for *artifacts*, the things, including garbage, that our ancestors left behind. An archaeologist digging at a prehistoric site where humans lived 20,000 years ago would most likely find broken pieces of stone tools, remains of food and charcoal from campfires, lots of shells, and plenty of animal bones—all garbage! It is hard to imagine that these prehistoric hunters and gatherers could possibly leave that much garbage, but it is true.

For instance, Native Americans living along the coast relied mostly on shellfish (such as clams and oysters) for food but had no use for most of the shells. They threw these away, creating large piles or mounds that archaeologists call *shell middens*. At some archaeological digs, scientists have found middens containing many tons of shells.

Besides animal remains, much of prehistoric garbage resulted from the making of stone tools. A stone tool is made by striking one stone against another, causing flakes, little pieces of stone, to fly off. When archaeologists find these flakes, they can identify where early humans lived.

Each time an early hunter shot an arrow that only wounded an animal and the animal ran away, the stone arrowhead would have to be replaced. To make a new arrowhead, the hunter started with a rock at least as big as your fist. That meant that most of the rock had to be flaked away to get the right shape and size of the arrowhead (Figure 9.1).

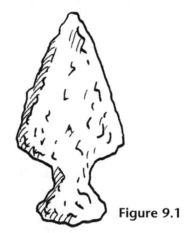

Figure 9.1

Nature's Garbage

Why do archaeologists have to dig deep holes to find artifacts and why are the treasures of the past buried in the earth? If you have ever been to the forest, you know that every autumn, lots of leaves drop from trees. With no one to rake them up they lie on the forest floor through rain and snow and the changing seasons. The next autumn, more leaves fall, adding thickness to the blanket already covering the forest floor. These cycles repeat year after year. Were it not for nature's recycling miracle of decomposition, the pile would soon reach to the top of the trees. What happens to all these leaves? Eventually, the leaves at the bottom of the growing pile begin to *decompose*, crumbling into tiny pieces, much like an old book or newspaper. Together with decaying fallen branches and trees, this material turns into *humus*, a material that provides the soil with nutrients, the food needed to promote the growth of new plants. Without humus, soil— which is made of disintegrated rock—would not sustain plant life. After hundreds and even thousands of years, new layers of humus mixed with windblown soil keep building up and covering whatever was there before. So if our ancestors had built a campfire 20,000 years ago, its remains would most likely be found today well beneath the surface of the ground.

In cities as in forests, the remains of the past are often covered. Great floods, sand and dust storms, or volcanic eruptions can cause buildings to be destroyed and eventually covered or built over with new buildings. In the large and very old city of Frankfurt, Germany, archaeologists found the ruins of old Roman buildings right in the middle of the city, several feet below the ground level.

Garbage in the City

As people started to move away from the hunting and gathering lifestyle and came together in towns and cities, what to do with garbage became a problem. With so many people living so close to each other, it was difficult to get rid of all the trash that collected. And while there was no longer garbage from stone flakes, these were replaced with garbage from discarded vegetables and fruits and animal and fish bones. Much of this garbage never left the city. It was often thrown out of windows and left to rot on the unpaved streets. There were no garbage trucks and no garbage dumps 500 years ago. Garbage made cities a dirty and dangerous place to live, especially during the period between A.D. 1300 and 1700, when a deadly disease called the Black Plague devastated most of Europe. Rats, attracted by all the garbage in the streets, carried the germs of this disease. People then caught this disease from being bitten by the rats or the fleas on the rats, or simply by touching infected garbage. The plague was extremely contagious, which meant that people who had it easily passed it on to their families and neighbors.

Almost all of the people who caught the plague died from it, so it was not surprising that many thousands of people panicked and fled from the cities. They had a good reason to be frightened. During the worst years in the 1300s, 25 million people died from the plague. As late as 1665, 75,000 people in London, England, died from the plague.

In time, town officials found that the best way to destroy the germs was to burn everything—including the bodies of people who had died of the plague. Luckily, by the 1700s, the plague was pretty much gone. But cities were not much cleaner. In New York City, for example, garbage was everywhere. Only roaming pigs and other animals did anything to clean up the mess by eating some of the garbage. Of course, in the process, these animals deposited their own fecal garbage.

Another big creator of garbage in the city was fire. Once a building is burned to the ground, all that is left is a pile of melted glass, charcoal, and bricks. All of this has to be cleared away to make room for new buildings. One fire just before Christmas in 1835 burned 700 houses in New York City. A great fire in London in 1666 pretty much destroyed the whole city. After an earthquake in 1923, large sections of Tokyo burned to the ground. Imagine the garbage of an entire city's burnt buildings! In the old days, more buildings were made of wood, which easily catches fire, and firefighters had less equipment with which to put out the fires. So fires often added ashes, burnt timbers, and fallen stone chimneys to the everyday garbage problems faced by people in cities.

Landfill

People living in towns or cities near water found a way of solving their garbage problem by burying it and sometimes creating more land for themselves by using the garbage as *landfill*. They did this by dumping dirt, stones, bricks, and garbage (including broken dishes, old nails, belt buckles, glass, and other junk) into the water along the shore. This mess was then covered by layers of soil and stone to make a flat and clean surface with no garbage sticking out from underneath.

For instance, the island of Manhattan was getting so crowded even 300 years ago that there was almost no space left in the good part of town, where all the shops and houses were located. The problem was that the island was about 11 miles (18 km) long but not very wide, and the early settlers did not want to have to build their houses "uptown," where it would take an hour or more to get "downtown"— to the shops—on horseback. So what did the people of New York City decide to do? Instead of moving to where there was more land, they decided to create land and solve their garbage problem at the same time. They added so much land that streets that were once on the waterfront are now a few blocks away from the river (Figure 9.2). Imagine how much garbage and dirt it took to fill in the water and then build houses on top without anything sinking back into the water.

Early business owners, who were very eager to have new land to build on, used almost anything to fill in the water. Archaeologists

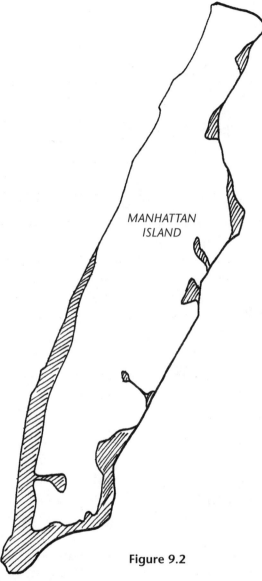

MANHATTAN
ISLAND

Figure 9.2

recently found most of a large old sailing ship that was used as land-fill. Even Ellis Island, the place where many of our ancestors first set foot in the United States, was made mostly of landfill. Only about three acres (1.2 hectares) when first inhabited, Ellis Island grew to 27 acres (10.8 hectares)—nine times as big as it had originally been—by the time New Yorkers finished dumping landfill into the water. After the disastrous 1906 earthquake and fire in San Francisco, the residents dumped all the burned ruins of the city into the bay, creating what is now called the Marina District.

Make Landfill

Discover just how hard it is to create landfill by trying this experiment.

MATERIALS

- 1 9 x 12-inch (230 mm x 300 mm) aluminum cake pan
- About 2 pounds (1 kg) of modeling clay
- 1 medium-sized bag of potting soil
- Some pebbles
- Small pieces of chopped-up Styrofoam
- Broken peanut shells
- Water in a liter container
- 1 small Matchbox or Hot Wheels car that you don't mind getting wet

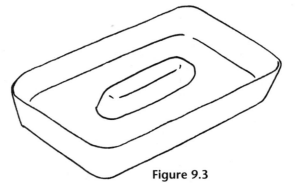

Figure 9.3

First, mold the clay in the center of the cake pan, shaping it into what looks roughly like a hot dog bun: stretch it toward the long ends of the pan and make its top flat and a little lower than the top of the pan (Figure 9.3). Do this until you use up all the clay. Next, pour water into the pan around the clay, creating an island. (Don't pour too much, or you'll have a flood!)

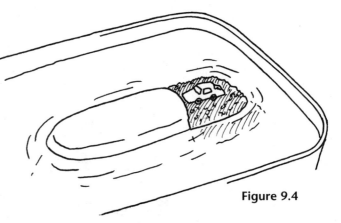

Figure 9.4

On one side of the island, use a mixture of soil, Styrofoam, small rocks, and broken peanut shells to try to expand the island. When you think the landfill is steady, cover the top with a layer of only soil. See how well you can make the island about 3 inches (75 mm) longer and sturdy enough so that the toy car can sit on top of the island without getting wet or sinking into the landfill (Figure 9.4).

As the experiment demonstrates, it is not easy to make land out of water. Imagine how laborious the process was before there were dump trucks and other large trucks to lift the dirt and garbage and dump it into the sea.

Dumps

A landfill at the water's edge was one way to get rid of garbage, but this had its limits. First, because landfills of garbage smelled bad and looked dirty, people did not want them near their homes. Some garbage also contains harmful bacteria that can hurt sea life, with the consequence that landfills along lakeshores or rivers can result in the death of wildlife. This is less of a problem on the shore of an ocean since the world's oceans are so vast; but, nevertheless, a garbage land-fill remains an eyesore.

The next solution involved people taking the garbage and, instead of dumping it into the water, just dumping it on top of unused land. This became especially popular after the invention of the train and automobile. Big trucks and trains could take the garbage far away from the city, where most of the people lived, and dump it in a big pile that could become 50 feet (15 m) high or more.

How Compaction Works

MATERIALS
- **Plastic grocery bag**
- **Assorted trash such as crumpled paper, used plastic food containers, and any other dry garbage you can find**
- **Measuring tape**

🏛 Fill the bag with assorted trash. Tie or knot the bag closed and measure its dimensions in inches: height, width, and depth. Multiply height by width by depth to obtain the volume of the bag, which can be expressed in cubic inches.

Place the bag on the ground and stomp on it, turning it occasionally, until it is as compressed as possible. Measure its dimensions again and compute its volume. What is the percent reduction in volume? To determine this, divide the compressed volume by the uncompressed volume and multiply the result by 100. Then subtract the final result from 100 to obtain the percent reduction.

Observe that compression greatly reduces the volume of garbage that has to be stored.

As time passed and cities grew larger and larger, people began living in the places where these old garbage dumps used to be—the same places that their grandparents had once thought was too far away to worry about. During the 1700s, Staten Island—one of the boroughs of New York City—was considered to be rather far from the center of the city on Manhattan Island, but by the 20th century, millions of people lived there, not far from where all the garbage was being dumped. Even today, you can smell the garbage if you are on Staten Island and the wind is blowing in the right direction.

Today, the residents of a city create more garbage than ever before. Added to the food wastes, there are now glass and plastics, aluminum cans, old newspapers and magazines, packaging products such as boxes and plastic foams, rusty old automobiles, refrigerators, and stoves—in other words, a huge amount of garbage. It has become clear to many mayors, governors, presidents, kings, and queens all over the world that dumping garbage may not be the answer to the problem. So now we try to *recycle*, to use again, as many products as possible and dump only those that will break down in the earth as the leaves do on the forest floor.

Recycling

MATERIALS
- **Notepad**
- **Pencil**
- **Bathroom scale**

First, look inside your refrigerator and see how many items have the recycling symbol on them (Figure 9.5). Make two columns on your pad, one for

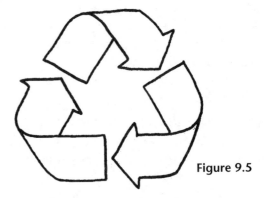

Figure 9.5

recycling and one for garbage. Make a check mark in the recycling column when you find something that can be recycled. Glass and cans can be recycled even if they don't have the symbol on them. Make a check mark in the non-recyclable column when you find something that cannot be recycled (most plastic without the recycling symbol). Write down what the non-recyclable item is next to the check mark.

Next, go into your food cabinet or pantry and do the same thing. See how many items are in your two columns. Is there a lot of garbage that you will be throwing out compared to what you can recycle?

Every day, before you throw something out, sort the garbage into separate bags of garbage, recyclables, and paper. Weigh the garbage bags, noting the separate weight of garbage, recyclables, and paper. For a week, keep track of the weight of these three materials. Once you have the totals for the week, multiply each by 52 to obtain the weight collected in one year. Imagine how many two-ton garbage trucks will be needed to remove all your garbage. What percentage of your garbage is recycled (divide the weight of recyclables by the total weight of the garbage and multiply it by 100)?

How can we make less garbage? Are there ways to reuse some of the containers in your house instead of throwing them out? Much of what we use daily is *biodegradable*, which means that it will decompose and become part of the soil. Most foods are biodegradable, as are many products made from wood or vegetable matter such as paper. But it takes a long time for these items to decompose. In cold, dry climates, a sheet of paper may last for centuries, while in a hot, humid climate the paper may disintegrate in less than a year. Next time you throw something out, consider how long it will be around before it is once more part of the soil.

Infrastructure Activities

Find out where your garbage goes after it is picked up. You may discover that it travels great distances. Call your sanitation department to find out where the dumps are.

Make a list of all the possible ways you can reduce the amount of garbage that you produce. Consider how you can reuse material instead of throwing it away.

How much room does all of your garbage occupy? Estimate the total weekly and monthly volumes of garbage from the volume of one bag. Note how much space is saved in a garbage dump because of recycling.

Pollution

When there were fewer people in the world, the smoke from fires disappeared into the endless sky; garbage deteriorated and was reabsorbed into the ground; and the waste from our bodies washed away and was diluted by the ever-flowing rivers. But now that there are more than six billion people in the world, the sky can no longer absorb the smoke; the ground can no longer break down all the garbage fast enough; and the rivers have too little water to dilute all the human waste. So what was natural 2,000 years ago now slowly destroys the sky, the ground, and the rivers, polluting them with the products of our civilization.

Pollution is the poisoning of our air, water, and soil with chemicals or germs, tiny organisms that can be harmful to our health. There are many types of pollution in our world today, from huge clouds of toxic chemicals rising to the sky from factory chimneys to the chemicals leaking into the ground from a discarded cigarette.

Acid Rain

In 13th-century England, people began to notice that the air smelled very bad, burned their eyes, and made everyone cough. People wondered what caused this. They saw thick smoke coming from the coal-burning fires used to heat buildings and realized that this was the cause of their problem. Before long, the English government had enacted laws to stop people from burning so much coal and to make them use wood instead. The people still were not sure why wood was better, but they noticed that wood-burning fires did not cause as much irritation.

Why is it better to burn wood than coal? Before we can answer this question, we have to understand what coal is. Coal is a fossil fuel that comes from plants and trees that grew millions of years ago in the soupy swamps that covered much of the planet. As these plants died and decayed, they were eventually pushed underground by the weight of layers of muddy soil that covered them. The heat and the pressure resulting from the decomposition and burial turned this matter into coal or oil that contained a chemical element called sulfur. When coal is burned, the sulfur mixes with the oxygen in the air to form a gas called sulfur dioxide (SO_2), which smells like rotten eggs. As this gas rises with the smoke from the coal-burning fires, it combines with moisture in the air to become sulfurous acid (H_2SO_3), a poisonous chemical. Clouds that contain this acid will drift and eventually fall as rain. The raindrops may contain some of this acid and kill plants on the earth and fish in lakes and rivers. This acid rain can also irritate our eyes and lungs.

Burning wood also gives off thick smoke that can be poisonous, but it is not quite as harmful to the environment as burning coal.

Following the new law, the English people in the 13th century started to burn wood instead of coal. But it was impossible for the government to monitor the whole country to make certain that the new law was obeyed, so many people continued to burn coal. As the centuries passed, all of England eventually turned back to burning coal as the supply of trees in the forests began to run out.

By the 18th century, the resulting pollution was very severe. Many people died of bronchitis (an inflammation of the treelike tubes that go into the lungs) and other lung diseases. England was already densely populated at the time and was where the industrial revolution began. The many new factories burned even more coal. Trains were also powered by burning coal that spewed carbon dust into the air. This resulted in acid rain that not only killed people but also discolored and then eroded the stone and brick faces of buildings. Not only in England but all across Europe, people saw the effects of acid rain. In Rome and Athens, structures that had stood for thousands of years were being eaten away by the corrosive action of acid rain.

The problem continues even today but a little more slowly because less coal and more low-sulfur oil is being burned. But if you were to go to the Black Forest in Germany, you would see that pollution is destroying the leaves and killing the trees. The Germans call this problem *Waldsterben*, or "forest death." In China, which has large reserves of high-sulfur coal, industrialization has resulted in increasing sulfur emissions in the atmosphere. This, in turn has increased the amount of acid rain falling on China's Asian neighbors. This is similar to the experience of the northeastern United States where acid rain has been caused by emissions from the smokestacks of the heavily industrialized Midwest.

Test for Acidity

How acid is your rain?

MATERIALS
- **Litmus paper**
- **3 cups**
- **Juice of 1 lemon**
- **1 spoonful of baking soda**
- **One cup of tap water**
- **One cup of rainwater**

Litmus paper has been treated to change color depending on whether the material being tested is acidic or alkaline (which is the opposite of acidic). It turns blue in the presence of bases (alkali) and red in the presence of acids.

Dip a piece of litmus paper into the tap water. Mix the baking soda with water and dip a piece of litmus paper into this solution. Mix the lemon juice with water and dip another piece of litmus paper into this solution. Observe the difference in the three litmus paper colors. You can also try some common foods to see where they are on the acid-alkaline scale, known as the pH scale (Figure 10.1).

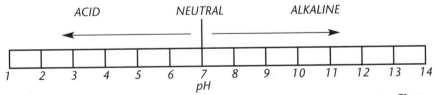

Figure 10.1

The next time it rains, collect some rainwater in a cup and then dip the litmus paper into the water. Observe the color change and compare it to the three samples you previously tested. Recently, some acid rain has been found to be almost as acidic as lemon juice.

Carbon and Its Friends

Acid rain isn't the only problem we face from the burning of fossil fuels such as coal, gasoline, and oil. The very air we breathe is becoming polluted. Though air is colorless and seems to be "nothing," it is in fact matter, that is, air takes up space and has weight. Air consists mainly of two gases, oxygen and nitrogen.

Does Air Have Mass?

Mass is a quantity of matter as compared to weight, which is the force of gravity acting on a body. Do you think that air has mass? Here is an experiment to find out.

MATERIALS
- **2 balloons**
- **3 pieces of string, each about 6 inches (15 cm) long**
- **1 dowel rod or wooden stick, about 3 feet (1 m) long**

Tie one piece of string at the center of the dowel. Blow up both balloons to the same size and attach a piece of string to each, then attach the other end of each string to one end of the dowel. Hold up the entire assembly with the center string. Adjust the location of the center string so that the dowel is level, indicating that both balloons weigh the same. Next, pop one balloon and notice how the dowel now tilts toward the end with the unpopped balloon. Since the dowel held in the center is like a scale, this demonstrates that the air in the balloons has weight.

Gases are light and therefore can float around us without falling to the ground. When you ride in a car, a colorless, odorless, but also extremely poisonous, gas called carbon monoxide (CO) is released from the exhaust into the air. Every year, enough carbon monoxide is released into the air by the United States alone to fill a mountain 3,000 feet (1000 m) high and 6 miles (10 km) wide. If that were to continue, imagine how quickly the whole earth would be covered with a poisonous blanket. Even today, the air is so bad in Beijing, China, that the average person who lives there loses five years of life as a consequence of pollution from cars.

Carbon monoxide as well as carbon dioxide (CO_2) are products of burning fossil fuels needed to energize our way of life. Cars run on gasoline. Coal, oil, or natural gas fuels electric power plants. Homes, offices, and stores are also heated and cooled with oil or gas. The result is that about a ton of carbon is released into the air from each of the world's six billion people. Even though plants breathe in carbon dioxide, there is no way that this huge mountain of carbon can be reabsorbed by the earth's green blanket. Therefore, much of the carbon that we produce stays in the air as carbon dioxide.

This pollution causes another problem, called the *greenhouse effect*. In a greenhouse, its roof and walls of glass allow sunshine to penetrate and warm the growing plants. The glass enclosure also keeps the heat from escaping even in winter. Just like a greenhouse, the earth's atmosphere allows the light from the sun to pass through but also keeps in the sun's heat so that life on the planet is possible. Otherwise, Earth would be ice cold like the planet Mars. When we add gases such as carbon monoxide to the atmosphere, it holds in more heat. The result is that the temperature of the earth goes up 2–10°F (1–5°C). This may seem only a small amount, but it is enough to cause problems such as a rise in the level of the oceans, which is the result of melting of the ice caps at the North and South Poles. If we don't do something to reduce the amount of carbon-loaded gas we send up to the atmosphere, the rising oceans could soon put coastal cities and towns under water.

As a result of global warming, glaciers all over the world are retreating and releasing their water to the oceans. Submarines traveling under the North Pole ice cap have also discovered that the thickness of that ice has decreased. If Antarctica, which contains 90 percent of the world's ice in a blanket over 2 miles (3 km) thick, were also to release its ice into the oceans, the result would be catastrophic. If just part of this ice cap slid into the ocean, the sea level all over the globe would rise by almost the height of a three-story building.

Changes are taking place that may improve the global warming problem, but perhaps not soon enough. Natural gas, which contains both hydrogen and carbon, burns cleaner and may eventually displace oil and coal as the world's principal fuel. It may take another century to decarbonize our energy systems, and by that time there will be twice as much carbon dioxide in the atmosphere as there was in 1900.

What About Other Fuels?

A small percentage of the world's energy is produced today in nuclear power plants in which controlled fission takes place. Fission is a process in which atoms are bombarded to release large amounts of energy (as predicted by Albert Einstein). If uncontrolled, fission can lead to explosions such as those in nuclear bombs. Obviously, fission needs to be carefully controlled. Sometimes, though, the fission reaction goes out of control and accidents such as the 1984 Chernobyl disaster or the 1979 Three Mile Island problem happen. These accidents poison the atmosphere and cause death and injury to many people. Therefore, nuclear plants are considered too dangerous to be used for new electric power plants. Worst of all, the nuclear fuel that is used to power the world's existing plants wears out and must be disposed of. But the used fuel is still deadly enough to poison the earth and the atmosphere. Governments have tried to encase these used fuels in lead and concrete containers and bury them, but no one wants them in their neighborhood. Would you? So, even today, this spent nuclear fuel is being temporarily stored until a safe solution can be found to bury it far from where people live.

Fortunately, there are alternatives. For instance, the heat inside the earth can be used to generate steam for use in power generators. But this *geothermal energy* is only available in regions of the earth that have hot springs that can be tapped, such as in Iceland, New Zealand, northern Italy, and Oregon or Idaho in the United States.

Another energy source can be harnessed in regions of the earth where the wind blows almost all the time. In regions such as the Low Countries of the Netherlands and Belgium and on the Greek Islands, windmills have been used for centuries. Today, giant wind turbines that look like windmills but with propeller blades can provide clean power where the wind blows.

Rivers that flow constantly can provide another source of energy, *hydroelectric power*. Such rivers are dammed to create huge water reservoirs. This water is then forced through turbines used to generate electricity.

Finally, there is a source of clean energy that is virtually untapped: the sun. If we could capture the portion of the sun's energy that reaches Earth, our energy problems would be solved. On a small scale, there are *photovoltaic cells*, which convert sunlight directly into electricity. There are also *solar panels*, which use the sun's rays to heat water that can then be used to provide energy or at least make the hot water needed in households. Of course, these only work during the day when the sun is shining. To have energy to use at night, a storage device such as a battery must be used.

The Power of Water

MATERIALS
- **Drill**
- **1 2-liter plastic bottle**

ADULT SUPERVISION RECOMMENDED.

Have an adult drill three small holes in the bottle, one near the top, one in the middle, and one near the bottom. Now, with the bottle in the sink, place it under the faucet and fill it with water. Notice the streams of water that flow out of the three holes. The bottom one shoots out much farther than the top one.

The reason why this happens is that water has weight and the water column above the bottom hole is taller and therefore weighs more. If water weighs about 62 pounds per cubic foot (1 g/cm³), calculate the pressure of the jet of water at the different heights below the surface. The pressure is the weight multiplied by the height of the water column above the hole. For instance, if the hole is 1 foot below the top of the bottle, the pressure is 62 pounds per square foot.

Dust

Gases are not the only elements in the air. There are also tiny particles of dust so small and light that they float all around us. Did you ever watch a ray of sunlight coming into your room and notice that when you blow or fan the air, you can see thousands of little dust particles drifting in the air? Luckily, this kind of dust is mostly harmless and can be filtered out by our noses when we breathe. Fuzzy little hairs inside our nose catch dust, preventing it from going into our lungs. But there is a much more dangerous kind of dust created by a natural phenomenon, volcanoes.

Our ancestors first experienced nature's air pollution when ancient volcanoes erupted, sending thousands of tons of ash into the air and darkening the skies, sometimes for weeks. It became very difficult to breathe and caused many people to become sick. In 1883, the explosion of the Indonesian volcano on Krakatau sent so much ash into the sky that sunsets all around the world were a spectacular red color for two years after. Meteors hitting the earth can also throw huge quantities of dust into the air. Scientists now believe that a giant asteroid $5^1/_2$ miles (9 km) in diameter hit the earth in the Yucatan Peninsula of Mexico 65 million years ago and sent so much dust into the air that many kinds of life could not survive, including the dinosaurs.

When anything burns, particles of ash are sent into the air. If you have a fireplace in your home, you can see a black substance inside the chimney called soot, which is incompletely burned matter. You may also see particles of ash (completely burned matter) that can accumulate on a screen at the top of the chimney. Soot and ash are the larger particles that result from burning wood. Smoke rising from the fire also includes tiny particles that are each 1,000 times smaller than an eighth of an inch (a millimeter). Smoke can contribute to *smog*, which is simply visible air pollution that can cause difficulty in breathing.

Other Pollutants

In Roman times, the pipes used to distribute water in homes were made of lead, which is the reason it is still called plumbing (from the Latin name, *plumbum*, for lead). For a long time thereafter, lead pipes were often used until it was noticed that people would get sick from continuously drinking water that passed through these pipes. Lead poisoning can lead to brain damage and death. People didn't realize until quite recently how dangerous lead can be, so, in addition to pipes, lead was used in paints, in gasoline, and in the glaze on pottery. Lead is only one of many materials used in our infrastructure that we have now discovered are pollutants. Because it is fireproof, asbestos, a fibrous mineral, was used as insulation on pipes, in suits for firefighters, and as a binder in floor and ceiling tiles. It turns out that the asbestos fibers can get into your lungs and cause deadly cancer. Fifty years ago, farmers used pesticides such as DDT to spray their crops. It was very effective in keeping crops from being eaten by bugs, but we soon found that it killed birds and helpful insects as well. Even worse, DDT could cause cancer in humans. Spray cans that are used for paint, hair spray, shaving cream, cleaning fluid, and many other applications at one time contained a very light gas, *chlorofluorocarbons*, also known as CFC.

Why Does Heat Rise and Why Do Some Gases Rise?

MATERIALS
- **1 tall glass**
- **Few drops of any kind of oil**
- **Water**

Put a few drops of oil in the tall glass. Pour water in to fill the glass half full. Notice that the oil seems to float on top of the water even though you poured it first in the glass. The reason is that a specific quantity of oil is lighter than the same quantity of water (oil has a lower density). The same principle applies to gases. Hot air is lighter than cold air and therefore will rise. CFC is lighter than air and will therefore rise high above the atmosphere.

CFC gas rose to the top of the atmosphere and began to destroy another gas called *ozone*, which blankets the upper atmosphere and protects us from the harmful rays of the sun. It is hard to believe that a little spray can is able to cause us such serious problems. But remember that there are billions of people in the world and therefore many billions of spray cans. Unfortunately, it is now a fact that there is a hole in the protective ozone layer that allows harmful solar rays to reach us, causing deadly skin cancers. Fortunately, the hole is over the South Pole where there are few people, but it could become larger and more threatening.

Modern regulations are helping us take care of some of these problems. Many pesticides have been banned until they are found to be safe for humans. Spray cans now use a safer gas. At present, when an old building is repaired or demolished, lead and asbestos specialists are called in to find and safely remove the hazardous materials. When you see an old bridge being cleaned and painted you will notice that the people are working in an enclosure. The reason is that they don't want the old lead paint scrapings flying through the air and into your lungs.

But breathing indoors can also be hazardous to your health. Picture this. You are visiting your mother at her office. As soon as you get there, your nose begins to twitch and you begin to cough. You notice that other people in the office are blowing their noses and sneezing a lot. When you ask your mother about this, she replies that the air in the building isn't too good. How can this be? The building's windows cannot be opened, and the air coming into the building is controlled. Well, that is where the problem starts. Air coming into a modern building is filtered and heated or cooled and then sent through ducts throughout the building. Unfortunately, the air passing through the ducts is never perfectly clean and may have some dust particles that will settle into the ducts. There is also always some humidity in the air that can allow mold to grow or bacteria to multiply. Worse still is the fact that some of the used air stays in the building, because only a small quantity of fresh air is added by the ventilation system. The result is that people might become sleepy, allergies and nose and throat irritation can become a problem, or dangerous bacteria can cause sickness and even death. This was discovered when many visitors staying in a hotel became ill and some died. Because the visitors were from the American Legion, the illness was called Legionnaires disease.

Any time floors are cleaned, carpets are shampooed, or walls are painted, it is hard to get enough fresh air into the office to make it completely safe.

If you visit an office building, you can check where air is entering or leaving. To do this, hold a tissue in front of a ceiling grill and see if it blows toward or away from the grill. This will tell you whether air is blowing in or being sucked away through the duct (which is usually located in the ceiling above the grill). If you live in an older home or apartment with windows that open, even when the windows are closed, air can seep in through the spaces around the windows or doors. Newer homes are built to be more energy efficient, which unfortunately means they are more airtight. Some people in very new homes are running into some of the same air quality problems as people in office buildings.

The Future

Trains that used to spew out polluting smoke are now run with clean electricity; cars that used lead in the gasoline are now lead-free, and some cars even use electricity; pipes that used to be made of lead are now made of steel or copper; electric power now comes at least partly from wind turbines; and the water that flows from our faucets is cleaner.

We started this story looking for our infrastructure. We hope you have learned how infrastructure developed and where it is now. What about the future? Since the world population is still increasing we can expect that the infrastructure will grow. There will be new bridges, new roads, new railroads, new tunnels, new harbors and waterways, new water supply and sewerage systems, new means of recycling garbage, new means of communication, and new means of generating power. We now send rockets into space with self-contained infrastructure systems. Nothing goes to waste and everything is recycled and sanitized. Why should we not do the same at home?

We are now living in an era of change to Earth-friendly products and recycled materials. The infrastructure will certainly grow; hopefully, this will occur without the mistakes of the past and with a concern for the earth we all share.

Glossary

Acid rain Rain or snow that contains high levels of sulfuric and/or nitric acid, which causes harm to people, plants, and fish.

Airfield A flat strip of ground used by airplanes to land. Before paved runways, these were just fields of grass, hence the name.

Anthropologist A person who studies the culture and behavior of humans and their ancestors.

Aqueduct An aboveground channel or conduit for bringing water to cities that became popular during Roman times.

Aquifer An underground rock formation that can hold water to supply wells with drinking water.

Arch A curved structure spanning over a space. It may be constructed of masonry, steel, wood, or reinforced concrete.

Archaeologist A person who studies the material remains of past human life and activities.

Artifact Material goods, including garbage, that ancestors left behind.

Asphalt A mix of coal-based products that is heated to a liquid consistency and mixed with gravel. It is applied as the top layer of a road.

Beam A single length of wood, steel, or concrete used to span from one side of an open space to another.

Biodegradable Capable of being broken down into matter that can decompose.

Biomass Plant material that is chopped up and burned or allowed to ferment to create natural gas and methanol that can be used as fuel.

Buoyancy The ability to float on water, resulting from the object having a lower weight than that of the displaced volume of water.

Cable-stayed bridge A bridge in which a series of cables that pass over a tower are directly attached to the bridge deck.

Canal A waterway built to allow ships or boats to pass from one place to another, often between rivers, lakes, or oceans.

Catenary A curve defined by a free hanging chain suspended from two points.

Centering A wooden framework on which voussoirs are placed before the keystone locks them together so that the arch stands on its own.

Cesspool An underground container for sewage.

Chemicals Substances that can be either elements, such as carbon or chlorine, or compounds, which are combinations of elements, such as carbon dioxide.

Chlorofluorocarbons Also known as CFCs, these are chemicals used in aerosol spray cans that are damaging to the earth's atmosphere. Many companies have recently stopped using these chemicals in their products.

Chunnel The railroad tunnel built under the English Channel to connect England and France.

Civilization A group of people who control an area of land, have organized government, trade, and a complex written or spoken language system.

Cog railway A mountain railway in which a toothed driving wheel in the engine engages a toothed track attached to the ground.

Compass A tool used to draw perfect circles. (Not to be confused with the other type of compass, which is used to find magnetic north.)

Compression The force that acts to shorten an object.

Condensation The process of changing a gas to a liquid. For instance, in winter, water will form on the inside of windows due to the condensation of warm water vapor.

Conduit A tube that can contain many wires. These may be located under city streets or within buildings.

Cut and cover A method for building tunnels that does not require boring a hole through the ground. In this method, the ground is dug to the desired level and a section of tunnel can be built or laid in and then covered up again.

Dam A barrier built across a waterway to contain and control a body of water. Dams are used in irrigation and to prevent flooding.

Dark Ages The period in Europe between when the Roman Empire collapsed, about A.D. 450 and when Christianity took control of the region, about A.D. 750.

Deck The part of a bridge that people and vehicles travel across.

Decompose To rot or to separate into simpler compounds or parts.

Density The weight of a unit volume of a material.

Dike (or dyke) An earth or masonry embankment built to hold back or channel water. The Dutch were famous dike builders, trying to hold back the Atlantic Ocean from their lowland country.

Ecology The relationship between living creatures and their environment.

Effluent The chemically treated liquid waste we generate that is ready to be released back into our oceans.

Electricity The force between charged atomic particles.

Electromagnetic wave A wave resulting from a moving electric charge that creates a magnetic field.

Elements Originally thought to be four substances—earth, air, fire, and water. Today, the elements are defined as the basic substances of all matter of which 104 have been identified, such as oxygen, carbon, and iron.

Evaporation The action that takes place when a liquid changes to a gas. It is often the result of the surrounding air being warmer than the liquid.

Fiber-optic cables Cables made of glass fibers through which light pulses are sent, representing digitized sounds or images.

Friction The resistance caused by the surface roughness of the rubbing of one object against another.

Funicular A mountain railway in which two cars riding on sets of parallel tracks and connected to each other by a cable passing over a wheel at the top of the mountain are counterbalanced against each other.

Geothermal energy Energy from naturally occurring steam and hot water under the earth's surface.

Gravity The force that tends to pull bodies toward the center of the earth. Weight is a measure of gravitational force.

Greenhouse effect The trapping of heat in the earth's atmosphere by gases surrounding the planet, as within a greenhouse.

Harbor A place with fairly deep water where ships can dock and be protected from large waves and severe weather.

Humus The highly organic top layer of soil composed of decaying plant and animal matter.

Hydroelectric power The energy created by water passing through a turbine that is converted to electricity for use in homes and businesses.

Ice Age The historical period when a large part of the Northern Hemisphere was covered with glaciers. The latest of these periods occurred during the Pleistocene epoch, which ended about 11,000 years ago.

Induction Discovered by Faraday in 1831, this process showed that magnets can generate current in wire.

Industrial Revolution The period from about 1800 to 1950 when machines began to take over manual labor and society moved from an agricultural to an industrial mode.

Infrastructure The basic installations needed by a community such as water supply, sewage and garbage disposal, gas and electric power, communication and media connections, and transportation networks such as roads, railroads, and airports.

Iron horse The early nickname for the steam locomotive. Since the horse was the most commonly used form of transportation at the time, people compared trains to horses.

Irrigate To bring water from its source to the area where it is needed.

Landfill A system of waste disposal in which the garbage is buried between layers of earth to create land mass.

Light rail Lightweight, quiet trains, usually electric, designed for use in and between cities. It is the modern version of trolley cars.

Lock A section of a canal with a gate at either end. The gates operate to keep the water from the higher section of the canal from flowing into or out of the lock.

Locomotive The engine of a train.

Maglev train A train that is held above a guideway by magnetic levitation (the repelling force of magnets) and that is propelled by continuously changing the polarity of the adjoining magnets.

Magnetism The force that causes iron particles to attract or repel each other.

Masonry An object built of stone or brickwork.

Molecule The smallest particle of an element.

Natural water cycle The earth's way of recycling water through rain, evaporation, and condensation, so that today's rain becomes tomorrow's ocean water and then evaporates, condenses, and falls as precipitation again.

Oscillate The term used to describe something vibrating or swaying from sound waves, wind, or other forces. Tall buildings may oscillate several feet on a windy day.

Ozone A layer of gas that blankets the upper atmosphere and protects the earth's inhabitants from the harmful rays of the sun.

Papyrus A reed plant that grew all along the banks of the Nile and had numerous uses, including the making of paper. It still exists in the upper Nile river valley.

Parallel circuitry A system of wiring where each bulb or appliance is independent and has its own branch that can be turned on or off without affecting the other appliances. A series circuit is the opposite; a set of Christmas tree lights in a series would fail if just one bulb failed.

Pavement The top, smooth layer of a road that allows vehicles to travel with little friction.

Percolation The passing of a liquid through a porous substance, like coffee through a filter.

Phonograph Otherwise known as the record player, it was invented by Thomas Edison and used a needle to ride in grooves in rotating wax (later plastic) cartridges or discs. The vibrations were amplified to re-create the sounds of music and human voices.

Photovoltaic cells Solar cells that convert the sun's light directly to electricity.

Pier A long platform made of wood or concrete that allows large boats to dock.

Plumbing The pipes that carry water to, from, and within homes and businesses.

Pollution To put into the earth, water, or air, harmful material or substances.

Pony Express A system of mail delivery from 1860 through 1861 that used relays of riders and horses to go from Missouri to California. The telegraph put the Pony Express out of business in a little over a year.

Precipitation The action of changing water vapor in the air to rain, snow, or sleet.

Pressure The force acting on a unit area of an object.

Radiator A device, such as loops of pipes, in which a hot fluid flows, that sends off by means of rays the heat from the hot fluid.

Radio A wireless device for receiving and transmitting sound.

Recycling Taking waste paper, metal, plastic, or glass and putting it through a reconditioning process so that it can be used again.

Reservoir A man-made lake or basin to store water. Reservoirs are usually located away from cities and are connected to cities by underground pipes or aqueducts.

Sewage Human waste matter.

Sewer A pipe or conduit of steel, concrete, or masonry to carry away waste water to a plant where it is treated to remove solids and harmful chemicals.

Shell middens Large deposits of shell pieces that were thrown away by Native Americans and other peoples in prehistoric times.

Silt Fine, mineral-rich particles that are found at the bottom of rivers and are often deposited after floods.

Siphon A tube between two liquid containers that carries the liquid upward because of the greater atmospheric pressure acting on the surface of the upper liquid.

Sludge Waste solids that have to be disinfected before being put into landfills.

Smog A somewhat poisonous mixture of fog and smoke that can irritate eyes and lungs, cause reduced visibility, and destroy rubber and paints.

Solar panels Panels that collect the sun's heat and transfer it to water for use in heating homes or for conversion to electricity.

Springing The base of a semi-circular arch.

Standard gauge The distance between rails in most parts of the world (4 feet, $8^{1}/_{2}$ inches). This makes it easy for trains to connect to different cities; different gauges require differently built trains (wider or narrower).

Steam The vapor produced when water is heated past its boiling point.

Surveyor A person who measures and marks off land for use in road, building, and bridge construction.

Suspension bridge A cable supported bridge in which a cable is attached to an anchor at either end and passes over one or two towers. Hangers from the suspension cables support the deck of the bridge.

Telegraph A device for transmitting signals over a wire.

Telephone A device for transmitting vocal sounds over a wire.

Television An invention that, through a camera, converts images to electromagnetic waves that are then reconverted in a receiver to images on a screen.

Tension The force that tends to lengthen an object.

Thrust The outward stress of some types of structures (such as a shallow arch) or the natural push of force toward the outside. Thrust can be balanced by use of extra support in the areas where the thrust is concentrated.

Tide The rising and dropping of the world's oceans due to the gravitational effect of the moon.

Truss An assembly of elements joined together as a series of triangles and made of wood or steel used to span over a space such as a room or a stream.

Turbine A machine that converts the energy of steam or water into rotational movement to allow paddles or gears to turn.

Tunnel An underground or underwater passageway that can be used to carry cars or trains.

Utilities The name for the various services that people use and pay for that require wires and pipes, including electricity, telephone, cable television, and gas.

Ventilation The exchange of air in and out of a space. A well-ventilated space provides air that is free of dust and bacteria.

Voltage A way to measure electric potential. The higher the voltage, the faster and more powerfully the charged particles move (and the more dangerous to us).

Voussoirs The wedge-shaped stones of which an arch is built.

Well A hole dug deep into the ground to reach aquifers where a supply of water is available.

Bibliography

Allen, Geoffrey Freeman. *Railways of the Twentieth Century*. New York: W. W. Norton & Company, Inc., 1983.

Bende, Lionel. *Eurotunnel*. New York: Gloucester Press, 1990.

Boyne, Walter J. *The Smithsonian Book of Flight for Young People*. New York: Atheneum, 1988.

Harrison, James P. *Mastering the Sky: A History of Aviation from Ancient Times to the Present*. New York: Sarpedon, 1996.

Lay, M. G. *Ways of the World: A History of the World's Roads and the Vehicles that Used Them*. New Brunswick, NJ: Rutgers University Press, 1992.

Levy, Matthys and Mario Salvadori. *Why Buildings Fall Down*. New York: W. W. Norton, 1992.

Macaulay, David. *Underground*. Boston, MA: Houghton Mifflin Company, 1976.

Macaulay, David. *The Way Things Work*. Boston, MA: Houghton Mifflin Company, 1988.

Rybolt, Thomas R. and Robert C. Mebane. *Environmental Experiments about Air*. Springfield, NJ: Enslow Publishers, Inc., 1993.

Salvadori, Mario. *The Art of Construction*. Chicago: Chicago Review Press, 1990.

Sandstöm, G. E. *Man the Builder*. New York: McGraw Hill, 1970.

St. George, Judith. *The Brooklyn Bridge: They Said It Couldn't Be Done*. New York: G. P. Putnam's Sons, 1982.

sewage, 89–95
  effluent, 95
  movement of, 92–93
  sludge, 95
sewers, 89–95
  shape of, 93–94
shell midden, 97
silt, 26
siphon, 8–9
sludge, 95
sluice, 28
smog, 114
solar panels, 112–13
springs, 6
steamboats, 24
steam engine, 22–24, 47–48
stratosphere, 9
Suez Canal, 22

T
telegram, 81
telegraph line, 80
telephone, 82–83
television, 87
tension, 59, 67
thrust, 65
trains, 45–55
  cog, 53–54
  elevated, 52
  funicular, 52–53
  maglev, 55
  and Mount Washington, 53–54

trams, 48–51
Transcontinental Railroad, 45–47
truss, 66
tunnels, 7, 49–51
  cut and cover, 49–50
turnpike, 37

V
voltage, 86
voussoir, 61

W
water, 1–11
  compressive strength, 17
  distribution of, 6–7, 10–11, 25–32
  mechanical means of moving, 29–30
  natural cycle of, 2
  pollution and, 4, 107, 114
  pressure and, 8
  pumping of, 10
  purification of, 11
  sheer strength, 17
  transportation by, 13–24
  treatment of, 11, 89
  wheel, 29
wells, 4–6
wireless, 87–88
  radio, 87
  television, 87
wires, wiring, 77–88
Wright Brothers, 39

Also Available

The Art of Construction
Projects and Principles for Beginning Engineers & Architects
Mario Salvadori
Ages 10 & up

Illustrated throughout
Paperback, $14.95 (CAN $22.95)
ISBN 1-55652-080-8

The Science of Life
Projects and Principles for Beginning Biologists
Frank G. Bottone, Jr.
Ages 9 & up

Illustrated throughout
Paperback, $14.95 (CAN $22.95)
ISBN 1-55652-382-3

World War II for Kids
A History with 21 Activities
Richard Panchyk
Foreword by Senator John McCain
Ages 9 & up

Two-color interior, 65 b&w photographs, 10 line drawings, 2 maps
Paperback, $14.95 (CAN $22.95)
ISBN 1-55652-455-2

Selected by the Children's Book Council and the National Council for Social Studies as a Notable Social Studies Book for Young People

"A special aspect of this work is the variety of informative activities . . . readers can vicariously go on a reconnaissance mission, grow a victory garden, track a ship's movements using latitude and longitude, live on rations for day, and experience other aspects of wartime life." — *School Library Journal*

Archaeology for Kids
Uncovering the Mysteries of Our Past, 25 Activities
Richard Panchyk
Ages 9 & up

Two-color interior, 60 b&w photographs, 19 line drawings, 4 maps
Paperback, $14.95 (CAN $22.95)
ISBN 1-55652-395-5

"An enjoyable history lesson and science project all in one." — *Today's Librarian*

"I highly recommend *Archaeology for Kids* for those budding archaeologists out there or for anyone with a curiosity about this science." — **Kathryne Natale, curator, Garvies Point Museum**

Available at your local bookstore, or order by calling (800) 888-4741

CHICAGO REVIEW PRESS

Distributed by Independent Publishers Group
www.ipgbook.com